AND THERE WAS EVENING
AND THERE WAS MORNING

AND THERE WAS EVENING AND THERE WAS MORNING

Essays on Illness, Loss, and Love

MIKE SMITH

wtaw press

Direct all inquiries to:
Editorial Office
WTAW Press
P.O. Box 2825
Santa Rosa, CA 95405
www.wtawpress.org

Cover Art *Moonlight* by Albert Pinkham Ryder
Author Photograph by Courtney Dean

WTAW Books are printed in the United States of America
on acid-free paper.

Library of Congress Control Number: 2017936590
ISBN: 978-0-9988014-1-4

In honor of Emily
and for Jennifer
and our five children

Contents

INTRODUCTION

MY FIRST WIFE EMILY and I were married for ten years. We met when she walked into the small bookstore where I worked and applied for a job. The manager must have hired her that very afternoon because we shared the following Saturday evening and Sunday morning turnaround shifts. It was fitting that we grew to know one another surrounded by books. She loved to read them; I wanted to write one. Emily had just moved home to Greensboro, North Carolina, from Washington D.C., where she had worked for a year or so as event coordinator at the Hotel Washington. She'd moved to D.C. after college so she could say one day that she had once lived in an important city. She rented an apartment in Adams Morgan and spent her lunch hour and weekends with the gorillas at the zoo. She read constantly, always her antidote to loneliness, and gradually figured out that she wanted to study religion as a way to confront the looming question of what she should do with her young life.

She would turn twenty-four the winter we met, eleven days before I turned twenty-three. At first we were merely new friends who liked to talk about books. C.S. Lewis's theology led to Emerson's aesthetics. Margaret Atwood's prose led to Dorothy Sayers's translation of Dante, which led to the novels of Toni Morrison and the poetry of Robert Penn Warren. After a summer of dating, she went off to grad school in the Bronx and that November, on her first trip back to Greensboro, I proposed. We set the date for June 21, six weeks after her graduation from Fordham University and from mine at the writing program at Hollins College in Roanoke, Virginia.

Conversations about the books we loved continued to ground and electrify our relationship. Our libraries followed us to the tamed mountains of southwestern Virginia in the first three months of our marriage, and back to Greensboro after Emily decided to pursue her doctorate later that fall. Those books accompanied us the next summer to Indiana, where she began the program in Ethics at Notre Dame that was to shape her thinking so profoundly. Our libraries expanded with our conversations, growing, sometimes alarmingly, in range and number. They went with us to Spartanburg, South Carolina, where we worked at our first teaching jobs, and back again to D.C., where the movers complained about their weight and number as they carried stack after stack up the stairs to our second-floor apartment. (I still use Emily's method of moving books by tying them together with twine—the brown-green ropy kind that wears its fuzz like a suit—rather than boxing them up.)

The next summer, after Emily's diagnosis of breast cancer and later, during her hospital stays that fall, I always kept a book with me. I rarely read it; just feeling the weight on my lap or against my side was usually enough. After her death, her friend and colleague in the African Studies program suggested that I make a gift of her office library to a new college in Nairobi, Hekima University College, with its School of Theology and Institute of Peace Studies and International Relations, whose students were in desperate need for scholarly books in English. The task of cleaning out Emily's office was one of many that seemed beyond me, and I happily agreed. The more personal books she'd kept at home, I packed up and shipped off along with mine to wait in climate-controlled darkness. It would be almost three years before I brought them out and brought them to bear on, and bolster, my mind once more.

Today, I have copies of Emily's own book to add to the shelves at home, should I ever move again. Sometimes, when I've come across other accounts of grief, I retrieve her book from the drawer to run my fingers over its cover and turn its yellowing pages. How lucky I am to have this object that is so much more than the usual talismans of the dead—a favorite shirt, tackle box, oft-used chair—and I cherish this small testament to Emily's large and lively mind.

It will always sadden me that Emily missed the satisfaction of holding the book's heft, just as she's missed the supreme pleasures of her son and daughter, their spurts of growth, the milestones and heartbreaks as common and unique as fingerprints. This sadness marks every new occasion. Since I can't see her delight in the way our children's minds skip, the boundless way their bodies transform before a growth spurt, my own joy is lessened in these pleasures. A record of how she hoped to live in the world, Emily's book argues for loving the strangers among us, even when they spring from our own bodies or the bodies of those we love, even when they are our stranger selves, and functions as a parenting guide for me. As my growing children become more recognizably their own selves, I wonder what more she might have taught me!

I was brought closer to my second wife, Jennifer, too, by discussions of the books we loved. Most of our early dates were spent on her couch talking while the older children played a board game on the dining room table, or ran around outside, and Langston, my infant son, crawled toward his afternoon nap on a blanket at my feet. I soon discovered Jennifer's mind was quicker than mine, and she possessed a generous soul that believed almost any subject was worth her interest if engagingly explored. She seemed to read constantly, and I realized that if I wanted to continue to engage her, I would have to begin reading in earnest again.

Although most days I try to resist wondering what Emily might make of this new life I've found, I like to believe that she and Jennifer might have been friends, that she would relish the very different ways our blended family of five children are becoming themselves. She would have admired Katie, our oldest, for her drive, and been warmed by Emily and Virginia's artistic temperaments and their interests in theater, photography, and writing, the very activities that had captivated her at their ages. When the girls' thoughts and behaviors seem inexplicable, remembering what she told me about her own childhood has helped me relate to my three daughters. It's pleasurable, too, to wonder what she would make of the two boys, their tender moments and their recklessness. I know she would have loved the bustle and noise of our house, just as, having grown up an only child, she always delighted in the lively holiday celebrations of my large family. She would have readily joined in the chatter and silly arguments of our suppers.

Seemingly plucked from an earlier time, my working life with its heavy teaching load, easy walks to campus, and the unavoidable intimacy of small-town living—one I'd never sought when Emily was alive—would have amused her. She was the true scholar, the person more naturally suited to this kind of academia. She would laugh to hear me routinely utter terms like "assessment" and "learning outcomes." Undoubtedly, she would have found, more quickly than I have, the connections between my new life in this small Mississippi college town and our years together as graduate students through our all too brief time in Washington, D.C., where for mere moments, it seemed, we lived the kind of life for which she had worked so hard. Emily would have identified with the resolve with which Jennifer pursues her vocation as a fourth grade teacher, and would have recognized our family's longing for stability within the frenzied activities and frustrations of our everyday routines.

Sometimes I let myself envision another timeline, one in which Emily is still present. I see her in some imagined corner of our round world. She's sitting at her desk, her open, lovely face backlit blue-white by the screen of her laptop. It's late, and her small family dreams in their beds. Her desktop holds messy stacks of printed-out drafts and books bristling with Post-It notes. If my mind holds the image, I'm able to zoom in close enough to peer over her shoulder. Through strands of bright blonde hair, I strain to read just what it is she is writing next.

August 31, 2016

My Emilys

Jennifer shivered and draped a white blanket over her daughter's shoulder. My stepdaughter, Emily, looked very pale. She was in pain, which made her angry. She would not meet anyone's eyes nor respond to their questions. She was eleven years old. The admitting doctors and nurses probably thought that they might wear her down, win her over, but I knew better. She had gone over a year without speaking to me because I made the fatal mistake of falling in love with her mother.

Jennifer and I had been married for seven months and Emily had been sick for the last three of them. First the flu, then strep, then mono. The mono led, finally, to an ultrasound to determine the state of her spleen, which seemed to be swelling at an alarming rate, an infrequent complication. In fact, the ultrasound revealed that her spleen wasn't enlarged. That afternoon, our family doctor explained to us that a germ cell tumor was growing from one of Emily's ovaries and protruding from her torso. She told us to choose a hospital and sent us home immediately to pack. Three hours later, Emily was admitted to St. Jude in Memphis, Tennessee, two hours by car from our new home in Cleveland, Mississippi. After admission, the attending physician told us that the initial treatment plan was straightforward: surgery to remove the rapidly growing tumor would be performed as soon as possible. With luck, chemotherapy might not be necessary. "Thank God for the mono," he said, smiling. Jennifer and Emily stared up at the ceiling. I was the only one in the room who smiled back.

The hospital room Emily and Jennifer stayed in those first nights had all the comforts of a resort hotel, including a television with access to more channels than we had at home. It was rarely on. They were on the second floor, the solid tumor wing. Everything was very clean, without the marks of heavy use that usually adorn the walls of even recently constructed hospitals. Our brief tour after admission included a stop by the twenty-four hour snack room, open to patients only, impressively stocked with food and drink marketed toward children and adolescents. By the elevators, a large balcony with tables and chairs for snacks and conversation provided the illusion of open space. A playroom for toddlers was located further down the hall. Nearby, a game room open only to teenagers, to which even parents didn't have access, was filled with arcade games, televisions, and a foosball and pool tables. The adult-free game room was a particularly nice touch, I thought. Maybe St. Jude *would* win Emily over.

It was a second marriage for both Jennifer and me. She had been the first person I met when I moved to Raleigh, North Carolina, less than a month after the death of my first wife. Not knowing what else to do, I'd resigned from my position as part-time Writer-in-Residence at American University in Washington, D.C., to be nearer to my wife's parents and my own. I found a cheap apartment and set about caring for my five-year-old daughter and infant son, Langston. Like my stepdaughter, my first wife was named Emily, Emily Arndt, and she too had been stricken with cancer, another in the set of coincidences of my recent life for which I am not grateful.

Jennifer had heard of what happened through a mutual friend and contacted me to set up a regular playdate for Virginia with her third and youngest child, William, who was the same age as Virginia. We kept that playdate every Monday for a year and a half before we began dating. One afternoon as I was leaving, I turned to Jennifer and said, "Virginia thinks we ought to get married, but I thought it might be more reasonable to start with dinner this Saturday night." Or something equally clumsy.

A year later, when Jennifer and I announced to our children that we *were* getting married, Emily ran to her room and wouldn't come out. Her reaction was understandable. Jennifer and her ex-husband, the children's father, had developed a comfortable routine of visitation. Emily and the other two children had only ever known one house, one school. All that would radically change. Two days after the ceremony, we would move our new family of seven more than eight hundred miles away, so that I might begin teaching at Delta State University, which lay deep in the Mississippi Delta. It was a daunting move for all of us, but, as far as the two older children were concerned, Mississippi might as well have been a foreign country. Only the two eight year olds, Virginia and William, were excited by the prospect—they would soon live in a state whose name they sang to spell.

Over the next seven months, as it became apparent that Emily was serious about this silent treatment, I was less hurt than bemused. Often, she'd miss dessert rather than tell me which flavor of ice cream she preferred, refusing to even nod her head until her mother, in exasperation, sent her from the table. I marveled at her will, and knew that, were I she, my need to please wouldn't allow me to have been so consistent. I wondered if one day she would appreciate the irony that this strange power of hers actually attracted me to her, that it kept me in orbit, curious to learn how she made sense of the world.

Part of what drew me to Jennifer, what continues to draw me, is the way she responds so gracefully to the events of her life. Manifest in every word she utters, every motion of her body, is her belief that existence is meaningful. She manages to convey this belief, somehow, without coming across as sentimental. Sometimes, I suspect her sense of self is almost completely instinctive rather than constructed. The moment after our family doctor revealed that Emily had cancer Jennifer buried her face in her hands and burst into deep, childlike sobs. When the doctor asked us to choose a hospital, Jennifer stopped crying immediately, courteously thanked the doctor, and answered, "Memphis." She stood and headed straight for the door, leaving me to scramble to catch up.

I knew that my wife was comforted by expertise, that she trusted process, and I wanted so much to reassure her that first evening at St. Jude. A heartening quality of tone existed in the voices of the doctors and nurses, something that hadn't been present in the voices of the doctors I'd heard three and a half years ago. These doctors knew our daughter would be okay. They were telling us this with each sentence they spoke and each they left unsaid. I knew because I'd been present in a room very much like that one once before and I'd listened to terminology very like the words that were spoken at St. Jude that night. I'd been present when the voices had no comfort to offer, voices desperate to stay as even as possible, as if one careless syllable might launch an avalanche of uncomprehending anguish.

"Will I lose my hair?" Emily asked her mother from the bed. No one answered. Only after the surgery would they discover that she would need three rounds of chemo. Though her prognosis was good, much more promising than most of the children she and her mother would meet during their stay at the Ronald McDonald House, Emily and Jennifer would need to remain in Memphis for at least three months.

During those months, I was, largely, bystander, outsider, other. I held down the fort at home, finishing up my first year of teaching and trying to placate and comfort the four children who remained under my care. Six days after Emily's initial admission, I returned to St. Jude for her surgery, and that evening, I took Jennifer out for sangria and fish and drove Emily's father back to his hotel room for a shower and a shave. On Saturdays, I drove the kids to see their sister and mother. Over those following months, I would make many such trips to Memphis, 115 miles from our home, due north, up Highway 61, and though the geography of the Mississippi Delta is remarkably flat, those trips would often feel uphill.

At some point during the calmer hours after Emily's admission, I remembered the most improbable coincidence of the small package resting on the bedside table beside my stepdaughter, who lay on the bed with her eyes closed. It had arrived in the mail that afternoon, and in the urgency and panic of the day, I'd just tossed the package on the van's dashboard. I'm not sure why I'd brought it inside with me, though I knew what the package contained—a copy of my first wife's book, *Demanding Our Attention: The Hebrew Bible as a Source for Christian Ethics*. Jennifer left the room to call home and check on the kids, and I opened the package.

The book's title appeared in black block type, like her last name. The cover design featured different shades of sandstone, a sober but attractive effect, with the faintest layer of large point script— Hebrew, I guessed—as palimpsest. Inside, the front matter included a dedication to our daughter and son, as well as forewords by the Biblicist Yvonne Sherwood and the ethicist Jean Porter, and Emily's own preface, written before she was diagnosed. Reading her words at that moment, her voice came back to me in such a palpable way that I was grateful I was sitting down. The very room contracted and I seemed to move outside of time; the sudden stress and worry of the day evaporated for the briefest moment. The unexpected lightening unsteadied me.

Until it was inadvertently erased, I'd kept a message from her on our answering machine for over a year after her death, though I'd rarely had the courage to play it—just as I had yet to watch the few family videos we'd haphazardly recorded. The phone message wasn't long, was routine really; Emily had called to make sure I knew when to pick her up from school. Reading the words in her book was better, hearing her voice in my head as her students must have heard it, as I'd heard it those summers of bright mornings when our daughter was at camp and we were both flushed with our work. Her tone in the preface is careful at first, strong with conviction, then, as she begins to thank those of us lucky enough to have been involved with the project, absolutely the warm voice of the woman I loved.

It was going to be hard for me to read any part of the book without slipping into memory. I remembered an evening when the end of her long months of writing and revising was in sight. I was already in bed, sleepily grading quizzes to return the next day, our dog, Jane Hair, sprawled across my feet. Emily appeared and asked tentatively if she could dedicate her project to our daughter, Virginia. The fact that she was almost in tears had struck me as sweetly comical.

Emily had just completed her first year as assistant professor of Theology at Georgetown University when, three weeks after giving birth to our son Langston, she was diagnosed with Stage IV breast cancer. Other than having her first child after the age of thirty, she had none of the ordinary risk factors and no family history of the disease. She died in 2007, on the first of December, a little less than three months before her thirty-seventh birthday. Through the effort of Emily's mentor and friend, Jean Porter, the book had been published more than three years after her death.

Holding its heft in my hands, I realized I might never have the language to say precisely what I felt as I turned the pages of her book for the first time.

Demanding Our Attention, as the book description will tell you, asks, "What can we learn today about human relationships from reading the Hebrew Bible, filled with such ancient stories as that of a father who raised a knife to slaughter his beloved son?...Focusing on a close analysis of the *akedah*—the Genesis account of Abraham's near-sacrifice of Isaac—Arndt demonstrates the power of even the most troubling and uncomfortable Old Testament narrative to teach valuable ethical lessons."

Emily's book began with her interest in the 19th century Danish philosopher, Søren Kierkegaard, whose work she encountered in 1998, her first year in the PhD program at the University of Notre Dame. I can still recall her expressions of excitement at this discovery, which strengthened her resolve during the winter nights she spent studying ancient Hebrew. Since its publication in 1843, Kierkegaard's treatise, *Fear and Trembling*, has represented a particularly important moment in the history of the interpretation of the near-sacrifice of Isaac narrative, and deeply influenced almost every subsequent commentary on the story.

In many ways, though, the scholarship of the first four chapters of Emily's book is prelude to her own reading of Genesis 22 in the final chapter. Throughout her studies, she had been drawn to the strange and difficult narratives that make up the Old Testament. Their familiarity was deceptive, and this realization led her to equate reading and rereading difficult texts to the ethical act of engaging the stranger. "In Christian ethical traditions, the 'other' has claims on us, has authority in our lives.... Relating authentically and transformatively toward others, loving our neighbors, can be understood as giving them critical and ongoing attention, even when they seem incomprehensible." Near the end of the book, Emily confesses that her long engagement with Genesis 22 has already changed the way she relates to other human beings. "Just as the concerns of the text and those of the reader, however distinct, are both significant and valuable in authentic engagement, so too is the concern we bring to the other with whom we are called to be in relationship."

In her introduction, Jean Porter captures something of the shock and grief with which those who loved Emily continue to respond to her illness and death. "Near the end of her dissertation, Emily writes movingly of her own experiences in writing the dissertation . . . I could not have foreseen that Emily herself would be the beloved child, the child of so much promise, whom we would be called on to sacrifice."

"Mrs. Arndt," Dr. Laurin said. "You have cancer." *Doctor,* I said to myself. *It's Dr. Arndt.* On the great chain of being, I was sinking like a stone. Later that day, when a nurse actually did address her as "Dr. Arndt," Emily wouldn't have it. *Please call me Emily.* Dr. Laurin, a specialist in hepatology, left the room to give us time alone. Emily seemed in shock. Over the next four months, I would never have the courage to say that I'd been dreading hearing a diagnosis like that since the morning after our son, Langston, was induced at thirty-five weeks and Emily's condition failed to improve as we were told it would. Three days after Langston had been discharged from the NICU, Dr. Laurin had performed a biopsy on Emily's liver.

Throughout her pregnancy, Emily had felt rotten. First, she'd been diagnosed as anemic, then with gallstones. Finally, thirty-six hours before Langston's birth, the doctors determined she was suffering from a rare complication of pregnancy called *fatty liver disease.* If discovered in time, the condition is dire for the child, but the mother usually recovers. The only remedy is to induce delivery, which, in Emily's case, the doctor did immediately, five weeks before the due date.

I spent the night of Langston's birth in the NICU beside my pink giant of a son, perfectly healthy except for slightly under-developed lungs and some difficulty latching onto his mother's breast. The NICU nurse was so astonished at his size and evident health that she couldn't stop laughing. Under the warming light, she showed me how to give him a bath and kept him out of his incubator longer than she said she should.

Now, Langston was three weeks old, sleeping in his infant car seat beside us in Dr. Laurin's office. Emily and I spent our ten minutes of solitude in one long, silent hug. Dr. Laurin returned to ask us how we'd like to proceed. "Please do everything you can," I heard myself saying, and she sprang to the phone on her desk, admitting Emily to the hospital right away.

Since it wasn't liver cancer, the doctors at Georgetown Memorial Hospital began hunting for the site of origin. For two days, everyone who looked at Emily's chart seemed able only to whisper. Finally, they discovered two tiny tumors in her right breast. These tumors, too small to be detected by a physical exam, had inexplicably and rapidly spread to what most doctors consider the most lethal destination, Emily's liver. Within minutes, we were assigned an oncologist who would plan and manage Emily's treatment. Dr. Liu, whom Emily was fond of right away, had the reputation of never giving up on a patient.

We walked the hallway from Dr. Liu's office in a daze. In the elevator, we rode down with a toddler sitting up on a large gurney and a man who looked like he must be her grandfather. The little girl was smiling and clapping her hands, heedless of the many machines to which she was tethered. Her head was bald, and large hearing aids awkwardly cupped both of her ears, and her face and arms and legs were swollen from excess fluid. The grandfather had glanced up as we entered. His kind face turned grim when he saw Emily's jaundiced skin, and I was struck again by how little I'd noticed her disease when it was so clear to others.

"Some things are worse," Emily said after we stepped off the elevator, and I knew she was thinking of our two children waiting back at the apartment. The older one had spent the last two days of limbo clamoring for our return and competing with her infant brother for the attention of their grandmother, who had driven up the day

Emily had been diagnosed. Parenthood asks too much of all of us. Sometimes it asks for the impossible strength to walk from a little white room on your own two legs back down the hall.

Dr. Liu was wonderfully compassionate. Part of her compassion lay in her frankness. She tried several times, I think, to prepare us for the fact that Emily did not have long to live. At our first visit, she told us that, statistically, only twenty-five percent of patients with Emily's diagnosis live longer than five years past discovery of the disease. She tried to tell us that, because of the strange way the cancer chose to spread inside her, Emily's case was atypically dire. Add to this perfect storm of circumstance the fact that Emily had just given birth, and it was a miracle that she'd lived as long as she did. I am still staggered by her strength in those months, the courage of her calm.

"Five years," Emily said at some point on our drive home. "Virginia will be only be ten. Langston will be the same age she is now."

The memory of that moment will not stop occurring to me each and every anniversary of her death.

Dr. Liu had scheduled the first infusion of chemotherapy for the next week, and the only thing Emily wanted to do when we arrived home was to give Langston his bath. We put the infant tub in the center of our bed so, after we'd dried him off, Emily might nurse him for the last time. The drugs she'd be receiving would show up in the breast milk, so we spent that week becoming used to the bottle. I think only Virginia was happy about this particular development, as she finally got to feel like a big sister. There's a great shot on my computer of her holding her little brother on her lap and feeding him his bottle, her mother propping her elbow to keep the baby's head high enough.

I spent every spare moment I had conducting searches online. I found a diet that was specially developed to help Stage IV patients and ordered organic berries from Oregon. Friends down south sent a Champion juicer, and I began to make stranger and stranger smoothies. I mixed carrots with blueberries for the beta carotene and vitamin K, and added protein powders, celery, and yams. Emily did her best to drink whatever I brought. God knows if it helped.

In the end, she would only have to suffer through the side effects of two infusions. Infections, including one that lingered for weeks in her infusion port, kept her hospitalized for two of the four and a half months left to us, and forced Dr. Liu to change her regimen of chemo. Within weeks, Emily became too weak for our evening walks. Yet there was her triumph of walking two blocks with a friend to watch Virginia and me make it to the top of the climbing wall on the day of our kindergartener's October Fun Fest.

"Is she really my daughter?" asked the woman who'd suffered vertigo all her life. She hadn't been able to rise from her bed since leaving the hospital two days before and when I saw her approach, I jumped off the wall, dizzy with pride.

Two days before Thanksgiving, I woke in the night to find Emily convulsing beside me in a hepatic coma. I called for an ambulance, remembering Dr. Liu's warning that the ER staff might have to be persuaded to treat someone in such advanced state of disease. Somehow, our children slept through the necessary commotion of ambulance and EMTs and woke the next morning to find our neighbors sleeping on our couch. (I believe they went to the zoo that day.) Reluctantly, the EMT personnel strapped Emily into a gurney and we made the short drive to the hospital. "Are there any other health issues?" the ER attending asked me. *Isn't that enough.* He was a bear-like man with a bear's beard, but he spoke gently. "Yes. You get the prize."

The next afternoon, Dr. Laurin, the doctor of hepatology who'd diagnosed Emily, surprised me by walking into our room in the ICU. "This coma is treatable," she said. "Her fluids are out of balance, that's all. I saw her on the list of admits this morning and wanted to come by." I felt like diving into the kindness of her voice, and was so encouraged I left to check on the kids.

Dr. Laurin was partially right. Emily was granted one last day of consciousness. I wasn't there when she woke that Saturday morning. In hindsight, I was so delusional about how badly off she was that I stopped for coffee on the way to the hospital, a choice that still keeps me up some nights.

Emily greeted me with a weak smile when I returned to her room. She was clear-headed and frightened when she realized she'd lost two days. The last thing she'd remembered had been the strange conversation we'd had before going to bed three nights earlier. I'd just gotten Langston to sleep and joined her on the couch. Emily's evenings at home had become fewer and farther apart. In the beginning, before the cancer and chemo wore her so completely down, we would sit across from one another and exercise, gentle routines designed to combat the long periods of inactivity when she was too unsteady on her feet to move around much. Emily called these routines our "dates." That evening, though, we'd both been too tired to do more than spend the hour holding hands, saying little.

Later, around ten, she'd asked me to help her put on a pair of socks. Except she found she could no longer say "socks." The word "boots" suddenly meant "socks" in her mind. Do you mean socks? I'd asked. No, she meant "boots." *Boots.* I remembered thinking, periodically, how glad I was that she'd been spared, for the most part, the symptoms of confusion and disorientation that occur when contaminants in the blood slip past an ailing liver and enter the brain.

How funny, she thought, that this scene was what had stuck with her, the only moments she'd been able to recall of the last two days. And she laughed right there on her bed in the ICU. One of her old laughs, full-throated and easy. The next evening, she became increasingly confused. Desperate, I asked her if she knew who I was. "Daddy," she said. *No, who am I?* "My love," were the last words she spoke. She did not regain consciousness again and died six days later.

It was near midnight. I was on the way home from St. Jude for the first time, after leaving Jennifer and our daughter Emily to the kind competence of the doctors and staff. It didn't occur to me then that this trip would become a sort of personal "Attunement." The word is Alastair Hannay's for the title Kierkegaard gives to the early chapter of *Fear and Trembling*. The narrator de Silentio speaks of an unnamed man who re-reads Genesis 22 his entire life, journeying many times with Abraham and Isaac to Mt. Moriah. In a footnote to the section of her book on Kierkegaard called "Renewing Acquaintance," Emily writes that she prefers the Hannay translation over the more conventional one by Howard and Edna Hong. She goes on to tease out the connotations of "Attunement," writing that the word "can mean 'bringing into harmony'" or the process of discovering a new awareness or responsiveness. "At the very least," she claims, "Attunement may suggest that these stories are a necessary 'tuning up'...."

I *did* feel tuned up, beaten, over-burdened. During the following months, as the stresses of work and travel and separation occasionally became too much for me, I would be the donkey, the servant, the knife. Arguments were inevitable, I suppose, but the fact that Jennifer would have to suffer most of my cutting would shame me once our family had regrouped and life together began to resemble what it ought to be.

In this same section of her book, Emily claims that "[a] somewhat bolder reading...might...suggest that Kierkegaard is putting his primary reading in the context of many others to achieve harmony or accord." As I drove home that night, I wondered how many trips like that I would need to reach harmony in my own life. Of the four readings of the "Attunement," not one has a happy ending. Not for Abraham, Isaac, or the unnamed reader/witness of these stories. "Every time he came home from a journey to the mountain he collapsed in weariness."

It was very late and I was jittery from coffee and the events and revelations of the day. I wasn't yet used to the way darkness takes over so completely in the Delta. Highway 61 can be a dangerous road to travel at night, but that wasn't my concern. I was thinking that it was a peculiar hell indeed to be despised by that young girl sleeping her first night in a hospital bed far from home. She seemed to hate me almost as much as she hated herself, her own maturing body, of which, nevertheless, she couldn't help but study every pouting glimpse.

Like my own life then, her life must have seemed very much like an alien text she couldn't read. Even as I put mile after mile between us, I couldn't see that this anger radiating toward me would eventually fade; that she wasn't burning with rage, but frozen with fear; that coldness has a bottom. At some point over the next two years, between treatment and the slow, unsteady reintroduction of what passes in our country for a normal adolescence, Emily would reach absolute zero and begin to warm back to her life.

Two years later, I would finally be able to begin to write about the very different loves I feel for my two Emilys and how terribly and surprisingly they continued to relate to one another in my mind. I couldn't see it then, but in two years' time I would pick her up from soccer practice and she would enter the car in a loud, teenage rush of chatter and complaint, overloaded with the accouterments of school and sport. At some point during that late winter, it would occur to me that I was no longer the primary object of her scorn, and hadn't been, not really, for some time. I had, in fact, become a silent co-conspirator, ally against the other aggravations that beset a thirteen-year old girl: the ridiculous demands of her coach and teachers, the idiocy of her classmates.

Emily would have to return to St. Jude every three months, then every six months, then once a year for scans (once a patient, always a patient at this remarkable place), but these trips would eventually lose most of the worry I carried with me.

Driving back home through the deep darkness of the Mississippi Delta that first night, I thought of the four children waiting for me. Weary as I was, I felt lonely and far from sleep. I even half-hoped one of the kids might wake as I thanked and paid the sitter, who had generously agreed to stay as long as necessary.

It was a selfish wish. One hundred miles away, my stepdaughter was struggling to sleep through her pain and fear. When I left, she curled on her side, facing the closed blinds of the window, pointedly away from the door. The white blankets wound tightly around her, feeble shields against the routine interruptions of the night staff. Her mother sat in the chair beside her, gently patting her back. I guessed that Jennifer would not shut her eyes that night, the events of the day and their implications returning like urgent whispers in an unfamiliar language.

The scene had been too much for me, and I'd grown anxious for the dullness of the drive home. What comfort could I offer? Three and a half years ago, I'd sat night after night in that same kind of chair, wrecked and helpless, hearing those whispers myself.

GIFTS SHE NAMED MINE

EMILY AND I WERE CELEBRATING our tenth wedding anniversary. It was June 17th, a Sunday, four days before the actual date, but we were celebrating nonetheless and went to see a matinee performance of *The Tempest* at the wonderfully intimate Elizabethan theater of The Great Hall of the Folger Library. She was seven and a half months pregnant, due the second of August, and had been feeling terrible. Her symptoms kept changing, bringing fresh discomforts almost daily. Some days, she lacked the energy to eat. Earlier, in March, her obstetrician had put her on partial bed rest, and she left the apartment only to teach and, sometimes, to watch Virginia, our four-year-old daughter, play on the small field across the street from where we lived in D.C. Since the summer break, things had eased a little, and even on bad days we were able to summon the energy to grow excited again about the arrival of our son.

During the intermission, we stretched our legs. I got us both a drink in the lobby, and went to find Emily, who was well ahead of me amid the throngs of people that packed the hall. Despite the impressiveness of the space's high arched ceiling and stained glass windows that drew my eyes, I spotted her immediately, looking intently at one of the glass display cases that lined the long walls. She was lovely, and as big around as my mood.

The Tempest had always been my favorite play, and from the first time I read it, really read it, I wanted to identify, to be identified with Prospero, Shakespeare's portrait of the supreme artist, the character who also happens to be his portrait of the supreme parent. Not until I taught the play as part of a survey course at American the previous fall did I pick up on just how much our hero withholds from the children under his care: his daughter Miranda, his future son-in-law Ferdinand, and the despised one he claims as his own, Caliban. As it happens often in life, the arrogance of parental prerogative masquerades as prudence and wisdom and goes unchallenged in the play. That Sunday, this aspect of Prospero's character leapt off of the stage at me. Imagining how Virginia, my five-year-old daughter would handle Prospero's refusal to share his plans with her, I found myself inwardly chuckling.

Emily and I had been married at St. Pius X church in our hometown of Greensboro, North Carolina. The building, sadly, is no more, replaced with a much larger parish hall five or so years ago—yet another touchstone lost from a life I no longer know. The week after we were married, we moved two hours north to Roanoke, Virginia, where we enjoyed a honeymoon of spotty employment for about three months. I'd enrolled in the Writing Program at Hollins College the year before, and though I lived five miles outside of Roanoke during that year, I fell in love with the downtown. We found a cheap first-floor apartment, two blocks from Highland Park with its large grassy hills and just within walking distance of the charming outdoor city market, a neck and shoulders of stalls under yellow awnings at the cross-section of two downtown streets. We were both fresh out of Master's programs and the plan was to work shit jobs and write, putting off larger decisions about our future for as long as we could.

In the end, we moved back to Greensboro, so we could work less shitty jobs near old friends, and so that Emily could start the process of applying to PhD programs. The only lasting memento we took with us from that strange interlude was our dog, Jane Hair, a lab mix epitome of an unofficial breed in those parts, whom I promptly baptized in the James River.

Jane Hair was our wedding present to each other, and now on our tenth anniversary, it seemed we were giving each other another family member. Only we hadn't yet thought of a name for our baby boy.

This naming business had caused us trouble five years before with our daughter's birth. Just hours after Virginia had been born, I was fumbling over the cellphone we'd finally broken down and bought for just this occasion, trying to call my parents, when I realized I still didn't know what to call the pink lump sleeping against her mother's chest. Virginia's birth had been a natural one, so Emily was still enjoying the postnatal endorphins our birth coach had promised her. I felt as though I could see the pain and anxiety of the last forty hours dissipating when she calmly reached out a hand to still my fingers on the phone, and said, "How about we call her Virginia? Virginia Marguerite Arndt Smith?" *Virginia* came from my mother and grandmother and *Marguerite* from Emily's paternal grandmother. The name seemed right the instant Emily spoke it.

I would think of the moment two years later when Virginia was a chatty toddler, stockpiling words by the dozen. One evening, her grandmother gave her a doll while we were shopping at one of those stores where every invention in the world is stowed on a shelf just out of arm's reach. The gift was a whimsical, spontaneous one, without occasion, and we hadn't left the parking lot before her Nannah asked her what she wanted to call the doll. Inspiration struck my daughter much the way it had always struck Emily. Without hesitation, Virginia, who'd been looking out the window at the vehicles coming and going in the lot, said "Truck!" *Truck*, of course, stuck.

Approaching Emily in the Great Hall, cold drinks in hand, I took my time. Hands wrapped around her stomach and gaze fixed on the glass display before her, she was intent about something. Those days, when she was well enough, she continued the process of revising her dissertation, and with the pressure on for both of us to make things work in our new city, I knew too well the minor tragedy of being interrupted mid-thought. The most stubborn problems often only allow themselves to be resolved when you have no time, no pen and pad to jot down your new-found understandings. Emily had always been a better sport than I about the inevitable intrusions on our attentions, but I was not going to risk disturbing her. After the play, we were going out for an early supper and I did not want to do anything to tarnish our golden afternoon.

I took my time navigating the crowds. Could there really be this many goodly creatures come to see Shakespeare on a beautiful summer

Sunday afternoon? When I reached Emily, I nudged her with my elbow. She turned with a sly smile and placed her hand lightly on my wrist. The warmth of her resting fingers seeped through the fabric of my shirt. "What about Langston?"

I looked down and saw centered in the display case a letter to the Director of the Folger Library from Langston Hughes. Hughes was asking for advice and assistance in organizing a Shakespeare festival in Harlem. Like with our first child when she'd suggested Virginia's name, I knew this name was exactly right for our second child, our boy.

Eleven days later, Langston Nathaniel Arndt Smith was born, a thirty-five-week old baby in perfect health, except for his young lungs. He screamed immediately upon entering the world, which was taken as a good sign, though the nurses rushed him to the neonatal intensive care unit and submitted him to a battery of tests. The fear was that he'd been born with a dire metabolic disorder, one of the consequences of fatty liver of pregnancy, with which Emily had finally been diagnosed. I went with him, leaving Emily to try to sleep for the first time in more than two days. Her doctor had induced labor to alleviate Emily's alarming symptoms of what was thought to be fatty liver disease, what would turn out to be the last in a series of tragic misdiagnoses.

Because Pitocin—a drug that had been given Emily to induce her labor—doesn't replicate but only mimics the body's labor-inducing hormones, the contractions a woman feels under the medicine are stronger and occur with greater frequency than with natural childbirth. Because time was of the essence, the doctor didn't give Emily painkillers early enough before active labor to compensate for the unnaturally intense contractions. The depth of courage she displayed over those forty-eight hours continues to astonish me. Yet, even though she seemed to feel better immediately after giving birth, something was still very wrong.

My son was one day old, sleeping in his incubator two floors up. Virginia was with friends, twin girls to whom she will remain devoted no matter how many miles I put between them. I was resting with my wife in her hospital bed, thinking how difficult it had all been, how much easier it would be once we arrived home and resume dream-life we'd began the year before when Emily accepted the job in the Theology Department at Georgetown and I picked up—from some minister of Fate, one mere month before the semester had begun—a part-time gig at American University. What I couldn't see then was that this was just intermission, prelude to what would follow.

Langston was the star of Georgetown Hospital's NICU, the biggest and healthiest baby by far. After the nurse took his blood, I was able to participate in his bath. Here was my handsome boy, squirming in my arms five weeks before I'd expected him, looking no smaller than his sister had looked after her full-term delivery, three long days overdue. As I dressed him in the white cotton preemie wrap hospitals provide and swaddled him in his blanket, I hoped his mother was already dreaming.

It was evident from the start that Langston would not need to be in the NICU unit long, and I soon realized that the nurses went out of their way just for a glimpse of him. His very presence must have been restorative for them, for the NICU was a nerve-shredding place. So many babies were hooked up to so many machines. There were so many alarms, so much heartbreak. The child beside Langston had been born at twenty-four weeks; he crashed and was brought back four times that first night I stayed beside my son, a number that I soon learned was typical. A nurse told me that his parents could no longer stand to visit more than once a week.

After five days, it was clear that the only thing keeping Langston in the NICU was his difficulty latching onto a bottle. We were moved to the room across the hall, where babies went to prep for going home. The night before he was discharged, I thought again of the day Emily had found his name, which made me think of the Caliban to whom I had been introduced four weeks before.

> Thou strokedst me, and made much of me;
> Wouldst give me
> Water with berries in it; and teach me how
> To name the bigger light, and how the less
> That burn by day and night.

Delighting in Prospero's assured command of the final act of the play, his power to bring about perfect destinies for his child, his capacity for forgiveness, I felt that I'd also be able to shelter my family from life's winds and set my children well-prepared on their lives' paths. I was wrong. My wife would die while I was dreaming beside her. Virginia will feel this loss all her life, her deep well of memory both consolation and torture. She will realize that the world, even those who pass nearest her, will not always be able or willing to see that her grief never leaves. It will stay in its elliptical orbit, returning to affect her at both predictable and surprising moments. Every sadness will gravitate toward this ultimate one; every jaunt of joy will be moored by this pain. Langston will know his mother only through a knowing that lies deeper than memory—instinct and imprint. The pictures he sees and the stories his family tells him, growing up, will solidify these indelible impressions. He will remember his mother only as others knew her.

That afternoon of our anniversary celebration, after the play ended Emily and I, content that our unborn son now had his name, sat silently in our seats, among the last patrons to leave the theater. She walked slowly, but steadily. She walked the way she swam or swung a club or threw a ball. Never an athlete, she was a master of form, nevertheless. As always, I followed her lead, admiring how clearly she was concentrating, bemused by the precision of her movements. Outside, blinded by the bright afternoon sun, she grabbed my forearm to steady herself, which threw me off balance, and we stepped from the path to keep from falling. We were laughing.

One day during my son's second year, I established for each of the kids a photo album of their childhoods. In the photograph I chose for the cover of Langston's book, he seems impossibly small. We were home from the hospital, a Monday mid-July. We had one week before our world was broken wide open, before the disease that was killing Emily was named. That Virginia and Langston were born under the sign of the crab, Cancer, will vex them both for years. This coincidence will make a kind of cruel sense to them, and on my next birthday Virginia will ask me what the disease Pisces is like and whether or not it's fatal. Langston will want to change his astrological sign and wonder if he caused the cancer that killed his mother.

In the photograph taken that afternoon, Emily looks healthier and happier than in almost a year, though she has exactly four and a half months left to live. She's sitting beside Langston on the bed, half-propping up Virginia, who reclines against her mother, smiling dreamily and looking at something off camera by the foot of the bed—probably Jane Hair, who must have been barking at the flash as she barked at the workings of any electronic device that whirred or clicked. Langston sleeps in his infant car seat, slumped doll-like against the thick headrest, so we must have just arrived home.

The photograph is one of my favorites. The knowing look in Emily's eyes and the fullness of her mouth reminded me that moments of happiness, however frequent, always surprised her. I love the way the shadows of her wisps of hair trace her jawline and her head inclines playfully, the smoothness and length of her neck. Somehow in this picture I've captured that smile of hers that used to knock me flat. When she smiled like that I used to think she could tell me anything. I had my own private oracle, but I rarely asked the right questions.

It's hard not to look at the photo now without thinking that part of her must have known how things would come to pass, hard not to see her already turning inward. She's wrapped an arm around Virginia's shoulders and her left hand supports the back of Langston's car seat. Or is she pushing our children toward me, offering me these two great gifts she has named mine?

Hours of Lead

This is the Hour of Lead—
Remembered, if outlived,
As Freezing persons, recollect the snow—
First—Chill—then Stupor—then the letting go—

—Emily Dickinson

ON THE GROUNDS of Georgetown University Hospital, patients had stepped out for a breath of fresh summer air. Nurses and attendants in green and pink scrubs, seated on the low wall outside the plexiglass doors, were grabbing a quick, late lunch. I set my infant son's car seat on the brick walk and tried to catch my breath, grateful he'd slept through the entire visit with Dr. Laurin, who'd just told my wife Emily and me that Emily's liver was diffused with cancer cells, the first of many catastrophic complications of her condition. Dr. Laurin feared that the disease had spread throughout Emily's body. Before treatment could begin, the doctors would first have to locate the cancer's origin. I called our neighbor and asked her to pick up our five-year-old daughter Virginia from school that afternoon and to bring me some formula for Langston, since it would be hard for Emily to nurse him while she was whisked from one wing of the hospital to another.

Two floors above, the protocols of modern medicine were aggressively applied to identify the origin and nature of Emily's advanced disease. She had appointments for an endoscopy, colonoscopy, CT scan, and mammogram. Dr. Laurin had wanted to perform a biopsy within days of Langston's birth but couldn't because Emily's blood wasn't clotting properly. Three weeks passed before the biopsy was performed. The day before Dr. Laurin called twice to make sure that I would be with Emily at the appointment when she would reveal the results.

"Our daughter will be in school, but we don't have coverage for my son," I said.

"He's not old enough to understand. I think it's important that you're with her."

Still I hadn't allowed myself to read anything into the doctor's insistence and convinced myself that she was merely following protocol. Standard procedure.

One of the benefits of the protocols of medicine is that it limits your gaze, keeps you focused. Both patient and caregiver embrace a myopia of next appointment, next infusion. The future means only the results of the next panel. When Emily's kidneys began to fail due to an interaction of medicine, my spirits rose and fell with her creatinine levels, the substance muscle metabolism produces, and by which kidney function is measured. I memorized the previous week's worth of readings as if I were an ambitious undergrad intent on learning the repeating decimal places of pi. Medical data entered my brain as invisibly as cosmic rays. Knowing what I should pay attention to, learning to speak the language became something to do, a way of showing support. Once, when a new doctor rotated on and paid us the usual brief morning visit, he asked me if I was in medicine. "Up to my neck," I joked, fearing I was still sinking.

I've never been good at managing my time. Emily used to complain that I was born schedule-deaf, just as some people are tone-deaf. I seemed constitutionally unable to register circled dates on a calendar or to abide by plans. This inability to keep to schedule had caused friction early on in our marriage, but after a couple of years, Emily chose to view this fault in my character as endearing rather than infuriating. Or perhaps she silently gave up. Certainly, I hadn't changed. Ten years after our wedding, I was still capable of sleeping through a class, forgetting a dentist appointment, or misremembering the time I was supposed to pick someone up.

It must have surprised her to see how completely I embraced my role as her case manager. I replaced the books and journal on my bedside table with calendars, and nightly recorded our questions, observations, and concerns. Emily had married a man who knew how to get things done, who could make sure she arrived wherever she needed to be, on time, at any time, a man who wasn't afraid to ask anyone for anything.

The evening after Emily was diagnosed, my parents arrived to stay with Virginia and Langston, and I begrudgingly accepted my grandparents' offer to take indefinite custody of our ten-year old dog, Jane. "There's just no way you can look after Emily and Langston and Virginia and take Jane out for walks three times a day," my grandfather said. "What are you going to do, strap Langston in his Bjorn and take along his baby monitor? What happens when Emily starts chemo? What if she falls and you're traipsing with the dog through the park?"

"Fine. Take her!" I roared, allowing my despair to overwhelm me. I still regret how frequently I lashed out at the people who were only trying to do me good.

Langston, thankfully, was proving to be a regular sleeper, so I rarely had to engage in the marathon sessions of singing and rocking that Virginia, at the same age, had required. I think I must have said a prayer of thanks every night for this unexpected stroke of luck. Once chemotherapy began, I had the pegs of teaching, Virginia's school and art classes, and Langston's routine of feedings, naps, and walks on which to hang the schedule of our days. Every new addition or interruption to the ritual of appointment, treatment, side effect, and countermeasure might be fitted into this arrangement. Nothing was too much, each aspect of our new life only needed to find its niche in time, while the moments of leisure and pleasure from our first year were bumped one by one from the scheme. Gone were the one-and-a-half-mile walks to and from my classroom on the campus of American University, which had allowed me to drop ten pounds. Never again would I watch as the magnificent, eight-point buck paused at the curb—absolutely unafraid—to wait for a break in the traffic to lead his small family from one side of Glover-

Archbold Park to the other, like me, simply one more commuter trying to get where he needed to be.

I'd never been a morning person, but I rose with Langston around five a.m. to feed him, half-asleep, in the recliner we'd ordered for Emily during her second trimester, once the futon had become too uncomfortable for her. I would start awake an hour or so later, and if I was lucky, return Langston to his co-sleeper without him stirring. Afterward, I began the second routine of the morning, making Virginia's breakfast and lunch, and juicing whatever concoction I thought most likely to tempt Emily and do her the most good.

Three days a week, the woman we'd hired to watch Langston for three hours, while I taught two back-to-back classes, arrived around 8:30, giving me enough time to walk Virginia to her classroom. Evenings, Virginia, Langston, and I shopped for groceries or chased down prescriptions before Virginia's bath and reading time. I found that if I held Langston high up on the crook of my arm, he'd let me lie down and read an entire book to Virginia before he fussed. They grew used to going down for the night together. I sang to them both while dipping and swaying with Langston in my arms at the foot of Virginia's bed. Emily called this move "the magic" because, somehow, it always seemed to work.

By nine, my little household, including Emily, was usually sleeping soundly, and I had at least three hours before Langston woke again—enough time to prep or grade, pay bills, clean the kitchen and put away laundry, or respond to any of the dozens of phone calls and emails I'd missed. I tried to convince myself that I could do this indefinitely, live this new life that drove home so convincingly what a privileged life I'd lived before. *Let me do this forever*, I prayed. *Let this be the penance for my ignorance.*

Early on, I thought my prayer might be answered. After all, it seemed that the diet I'd adopted in solidarity with Emily, who'd been given strict, nutritional guidelines by her dietician, was paying dividends already. I was twenty pounds lighter than I'd been at my wedding and feeling more energetic than I had in years. Emily's first infusion had gone well, and I took it as a good sign that the most serious side effect of the chemo seemed to be fatigue. She felt nauseated at times but rarely to the point that she wasn't willing to at least try to eat what I brought her. After the tenth day, her strength began to return. As long as I didn't extend my gaze beyond the leaden hours of the clock, the tomorrows that rushed headlong to meet us, the world still made sense. If I didn't wonder for too long what Emily was thinking as she turned increasingly inward, I could manage. We all could.

Soon, though, Emily began to lose her taste for television, movies, card games, and, finally, reading. By September, even the books of her childhood, those beaten and boxed volumes of Laura Ingalls Wilder stories to which she'd turned throughout our marriage in times of sadness or worry, stayed on the top of her bookshelf. She marked time by my presence in our room, venturing down the hall only infrequently. As she weakened, we were forced to limit our afternoon family time to bathing Langston in his infant tub or playing with him on our bed.

Often, the side effects of the chemo and fatigue pushed her beyond sleep. On her visits home, only Langston and Virginia could rouse her, and, once she started spending more time in the hospital, only me. But no matter how rotten she felt, how tired she became, she greeted me with one of her smiles. Whether joining her in our bed at home or sneaking through her hospital room door as I did every night during her stays, to remain with her until morning, I was graced with a wide grin.

My life was formal; each day pre-determined. A good day meant every item on my list had been checked off. Nights were pared down, an emotionless response to regiment and event. No longer did the darkness offer itself up as possibility, mystery. During my twenties, in the early years of our marriage, I'd developed the habit of writing late at night after Emily had fallen asleep. Then I believed that my successes in writing, the private ones that mattered, occurred only when those dark hours remained uninterrupted. Now, those hours were for collapse. I no longer crawled into bed with a book, allowing myself the leisure of imagining how I might have gone about writing it—my personal version of counting sheep. Sleep was instantaneous, a feature of exhaustion, and tomorrow would be the same as the day before. Tomorrow was always the same.

The first time Emily and I arrived for her infusion of chemo, my fear dissipated as protocol took over. After the standard blood work was done, a tech escorted us to a large room partitioned by curtains into petal-like sections, each surrounding the nurse's station. Six recliners faced the center, and all were occupied. What dispelled my fear was the blasé tone of the room. The recliners might have been old-fashioned barber's chairs, their occupants waiting for a trim on their lunch break. Except no one spoke and there was no genial atmosphere of regulars well-met. Patients wore the uniforms of their occupations, and it was obvious that, for the veterans of this place, the day of their infusions was merely another workday. When the chemo had fully emptied from the IVs into their veins, they buttoned up their shirts, grabbed their hats or purses, and headed for the door. Their appointments might have been just another in the long list of ordinary errands.

That first time the man sitting across from us was reading *Sports Illustrated*. He likely worked in construction, his boots spattered with the light brown mud of foundation work. His face and neck had been ruddied by the sun, evident despite the flush that chemo causes when it enters the bloodstream. He caught me staring at the port on his chest and the long line of poisonous cure leading from it. "Fill 'er up?" he said, and smiled. My laugh was brittle and he chuckled. "She'll get used to it before you do," he said.

We waited for Emily's IV bag to be prepared, and the man's co-worker appeared to pick him up, a younger man both nervous and deferential toward his friend. They were headed back to work. Probably, the man had been doing this long enough to know he needed to make use of the burst of energy that accompanies infusion. Punch in. Punch out. I felt inspired, eager to embrace these routines of restoring Emily's health. I fantasized that years later Emily would simply schedule her teaching load around these necessary afternoons, treatments that kept her cancer perpetually at bay. Managing it. Managing to make it.

A month and a half after this first infusion, Emily entered the hospital for what would become her longest stay, and the following morning I witnessed another incident that renewed my hope, when it was most needed. We'd spent the night in the E.R. waiting for a bed on the Concentrated Care Facility of Lombardi Cancer Center, though trying not to think of what that might mean for the bed's current occupant. Emily's blood infection was being treated with Cipro, a general heavy-duty antibiotic that made her groggy, and meant we'd need to stay in the hospital until the exact pathogen had been identified and a targeted antibiotic administered. Emily had been feverish and dehydrated, and the Cipro wasn't working as fast as the doctors hoped. Eventually, she was sent to the floor reserved for immune-suppressed patients. An unexpected aspect of her chemotherapy was that it hadn't greatly affected her white blood cell count, at least not enough to classify her as neutrapenic, so unlike most patients on the floor, she wasn't required to wear a mask outside her room.

That first morning, while Emily napped, I left her room to roam the halls in search of coffee. Patients' rooms lined the hall, the nurse's station in the center. From the far end of the hall, a patient strode purposefully in my direction. He was about thirty-five years old, I calculated, my age, and imposingly tall. Hospital gowns seem designed in part to disguise physique, yet it was obvious that his body was exceptional, that of a competitive swimmer, perhaps. He was bald, of course, but he had made the look so much his own that I found it impossible to imagine him with hair. His face was a mask of determination, his steps driven, and he seemed oblivious to everything but the number of laps that lay ahead of him. I decided to follow him.

Nurses, smiling or nodding, scattered like sheep before him, his right arm pumping to match his stride, his left dragging the rolling IV leashed to him as if a petulant child. He was as relentless as the sun through the hospital windows. I left the floor to get coffee and when I returned, he'd gone back to his bed, where I caught a glimpse through the door. His laptop was open before him on the overbed table.

I asked the day nurse about him. "Oh, that's Ted. He's here all the time." A patient for years, he'd become something of a celebrity.

The relapses that brought him back were nothing if not expected, and the entire floor had come to count on seeing him with regularity. For two weeks, I worshipped his courage, and I convinced myself I'd been shown another example of how we might conquer through quarantine, cure by compartmentalizing this disease. The cycles within the larger cycles of days might become gears within gears moving us along this new path, the movement itself restoring, then maintaining, our balance.

Promisingly, the nurse staff seemed bemused by my embrace of the new order. When Emily's oncologist, Dr. Liu, had said the regimen of chemotherapy would be necessary for the rest of her life, I told myself she must have meant indefinitely, then forever. Who knew how long the chemo might keep the cancer at bay? I was present for every vitals check, every round, every consult when the team of doctors and students crowded around Emily's bed. I learned to administer the breathing test and treatment Emily underwent every day and I became so averse to the scent of Albuturol that, two years later, when Langston was diagnosed with asthma and I had to administer the drug to him, I had to will myself to hold his squirming body on my lap without retching.

As the oncology staff worked, I learned, regaling them with my new philosophy, built on the rituals and duties of preserving Emily's life and helping her recover her health. Somehow, I did not view these goals as separate. These were the building blocks of our new life together. Some administrations, like the routine of chemo infusion, would be with us forever, the iron struts at the center of our bricks, the constants, the essentials, which could never be altered or permitted to fall away. Progress might be measured by noting when the variable routines ended and began.

Between 10 and 11, the physical therapist will come by for exercises and to check off her list of questions. Her visits will end when you are strong enough to get on your feet. In the afternoons, right before I leave to pick up Virginia from school, the respiratory therapist will arrive to measure your breathing and work with you to expand your lung. Once your thoracentesis is performed, they'll show me how to drain your lung, which will help with your breathing and walking.

On this day, the antibiotics will drop off. On this day, your regular diet might resume. Let's squeeze in a short walk after clinic.

We can expect the aftermath of chemo to last three weeks. Immediately after infusion, you'll have the surge, so, perhaps, we'll use that time to return to your book. Days three through ten, we know, become increasingly difficult, so I'll stop putting the protein powder in your smoothies.

Octoberfest is coming up. Our neighborhood is going to block off 38th Street a block east and west of Beeker Avenue and roast a whole pig right in the street. This will give us, once you're discharged, two weeks to build up the strength to walk the distance. You can rest on Julie's porch with Langston while Ginia and I watch the guy who eats the eyes and brain eat the eyes and brain. Then we can go home in time for his supper and her bath.

On Mondays, I have to remember to place an order for a new box of 3 liter containers for your pleural effusion. I can't forget because if we run out on the weekend I'll have to waste an afternoon driving from ER to ER trying to bum a couple to last until Monday. I really wish they'd let me buy in bulk.

As Emily's long stay in the hospital lengthened, I began to think I could discern the personalities of the nurses assigned to her room. I analyzed the way they wrote their names on the whiteboard opposite the head of Emily's bed. Katie made a heart out of the dot above the "i" and left wide loops in the "K" of her name. She always wrote in green. She was young and nervous in a friendly way. She used the majestic plural and seemed perplexed that Emily didn't want to watch the television mounted high on the wall.

"Are you sure we can't find you something to watch?"

"No, thank you. Not now."

The lives of nurses consist of cycles within cycles, too. Four days on, three off; twelve hour shifts. Emily liked all the nurses, and managed a smile for whoever was caring for her that day or night. I preferred the older ones, the no-nonsense veterans. I didn't blame the younger ones for their whispering at the nurse's station, the breezy way they went about their tasks, the way they listened but didn't quite hear your concerns or questions, or their almost religious belief that protocol answered everything. But I preferred the ones like Helen, the veterans who must have known how bad off Emily was, who skipped the vitals check if Emily were sleeping, who treated everything matter-of-factly.

Once, when Emily was out of her head from a drug reaction and had spent the night trying to get out of bed, Helen and I were forced to hold her down. The doctor briefed me on what was going on. "I think it's the medicine," he said, "but I have to tell you that I've seen patients behave this way when they are near death."

After he left, Helen gripped my elbow and whispered, "He shouldn't have said that. I've seen that, too. This is not that."

A month and a half later, after that final hospital stay, it was Helen who let me wash Emily's face. The breathing tube and mask had been removed, and I'd pulled the bed sheet up to her chin. Helen told me to take all the time I needed and left me alone in the room. It'd been six days since I'd seen my wife's face uncovered. I went through this last ritual in a daze. I now know that I must have been in shock, but for months afterward, my inability to respond emotionally lacerated me—this last time I might see and touch my wife's face. The thought cut me down whenever my waking mind recalled it, unbidden.

If I'm honest with myself, I realize that my desire to perform this last ritual, this first step in how I said goodbye, felt obligatory. I undertook this washing to fulfill my own expectations of what a dutiful spouse ought to do. I sensed, even as I began, that what I was doing was not the loving act of a husband fully in the moment, as act of communion or supplication, but someone afraid of how he would feel the rest of his life if he didn't perform this final service.

My wife's face was cold already. The bilirubin that had been excreted through her pores for weeks yellowed the washcloth. I asked for another. I could not reach a place of tenderness. My thoughts were questions of a single nature: Can she see this? Is she above me, watching? Does she know my heart's not here but reaching out blindly toward the future and past simultaneously? Will she forgive me that this is so, that my heart is in search of itself, seeking any other place in time but this one?

What does it mean when ritual ceases to encompass and channel our deepest feelings? What does it mean when the fulfillment of protocol becomes end, not means? My hand went through the motions of blotting dry my beloved wife's face while the rest of me was as far from that hospital bed as she was. Why was that? Was that stupor? Was it letting go?

THE GALES OF COMING WINTER

Altho' the end of love was hers—
Fruition, Motherhood.

—Vachel Lindsay

DURING THE NORTH CAROLINA SUMMERS, I longed for fall. Growing up, Thanksgiving was my favorite holiday, the one without ransoms and responsibilities, the one occasion at which I felt I could be fully present, fully in the present, fully embodied in my corporeal self. Harvest time. The supreme pleasure of embodiment.

At the counter of the bookstore where Emily and I worked, I luxuriated in the slow spread of November sunsets beyond the storefront windows. After work, I'd walk the railroad tracks near my apartment, trying to spy my sign in the night sky. Nine months after we began dating, I proposed to Emily the day she returned home from graduate school to celebrate Thanksgiving. Seven years later, it was November when we discovered Emily was pregnant with Virginia, and it was just before Thanksgiving five years after that when we confirmed she was pregnant with the son she would name Langston. These days, my feelings about this time of year have so utterly changed that I'm befuddled when I try to remember the physical jolt of anticipation I used to feel come mid-September.

Two years, almost to the day, before she fell into the coma that led to her death, Emily suffered a late miscarriage on Thanksgiving Day. It was 2005. She was twenty weeks along in the pregnancy, nearing the cusp of fetal viability, and was exhausted. That fall, she found herself after two years, suddenly, chair of her small department at Converse College, actively on the market for another job, and preparing for the oral defense of her dissertation weeks away. On Tuesday, she'd just returned from an annual conference in Philadelphia, having interviewed for the Georgetown position that she would be offered later that spring.

Four days off from the grind of school would not be long enough to recover her strength, but she was looking forward to visiting my parents. They'd recently relocated to Wilkesboro, North Carolina, a little over two hours away north and east of Spartanburg. We spent that Wednesday hurriedly cleaning our dusty bungalow, then packed and drove—recklessly, carelessly—late that evening to my parents' house. The next morning, Emily woke to a sharp pain in her belly and discovered her underwear heavy with blood.

Abundance. So sharply now do my personal feelings seem at odds with the collective on Thanksgiving that it is difficult for me to function in any meaningful way. I go through the motions. It's become harder rather than easier to be in my own skin on this holiday. Time and distance haven't helped. Thanksgiving is a big deal in my new home in the Delta. The schools, even the universities, shut down for the whole week, which doesn't seem pedagogically sound and, as well, frustrates young new-hires trying to balance their syllabi. But in this region, one still largely determined by rural codes of conduct, Thanksgiving falls close enough to harvest that it would be cold-hearted not to give the holiday its due. Harvest time still means something here.

Though Thanksgiving is our most democratic of holidays, celebrated everywhere in the country and by everyone, there's something about this holiday that makes it seem southern. Tourist agencies in Virginia have for years aimed to supplant Plymouth Rock with an earlier meal at Jamestown and thereby lay claim to the first Thanksgiving. Does the South's celebration of Thanksgiving belie a desire to shift the cultural memory? Does the celebration between European settlers and the Wampanog tribe seem somehow akin to contemporary race relations between whites and African Americans in southern towns still too often divided by color? In what sense does Thanksgiving justify economic privilege? In what sense does it celebrate rural wealth and the manipulation of natural resources, rich expanses of land and livestock unjustly divided?

Surprising, then, to recall that Langston Hughes, my early hero and the poet for whom my son is named, an African-American writer who wrestled so eloquently and thoughtfully with the legacy of Jim Crow, should treat Thanksgiving so straightforwardly in his early work. His poem, "Thanksgiving Time," reads like a radio jingle. The last quatrain is enough to show what I mean.

When the gales of coming winter outside your window howl,
When the air is sharp and cheery so it drives away your scowl,
When one's appetite craves turkey and will have no other fowl,
It's Thanksgiving Time!

Of course, Hughes wrote this poem before he was twenty years old and, in the *Collected Poems*, it appears in the appendix "Poetry for Children," appearing the same year as one of his most anthologized poems, "The Negro Speaks of Rivers." He dealt with Thanksgiving in prose form even earlier, in his youth, writing an overly earnest story on the subject. "Those Who Have No Turkey" has, at least, an admirable ethos and evokes the pleasing theme that wealth might limit our capacity for gratitude, just as wealth can stunt a tendency to behave graciously toward others.

It was in November, more than eighty years before Emily, Virginia, and I moved to Washington D.C. that Hughes arrived from England with only the coat on his back. A year later, he was working at the Wardman Park Hotel where he happened to have the good luck to see the poet Vachel Lindsey sit down for a meal. Lindsay, already famous as a troubadour-poet traveling the country trading poems for bread, famously publicized Hughes's work, which brought Hughes to the attention of the white reading public. Though "The Negro Speaks of Rivers" had already been published in *Crisis* four years before, the move back to the States proved fortuitous to his career. Lindsay, who was born in 1879, took his own life by drinking a bottle of Lysol fifty-two years later, and is these days admired more than he is read. His books are no longer commercially published. He isn't taught in schools, though a person might, on occasion, still hear a poem of his recited on the radio. I know no Thanksgiving poem of his, per se, but this section of his "Sweethearts of the Year," subtitled "Sweetheart Autumn," seems apropos:

> The woods were black and crimson,
> The frost-bit flowers were dead,
> But Sweetheart Indian Summer came
> With love-winds round her head.
> While fruits God-given and splendid
> Belonged to her domain:
> Baskets of corn in perfect ear
> And grapes with purple stain...

This section of the poem ends with the two lines I have appropriated as an epigraph to this essay, as my title is lifted from the last stanza of Hughes's poem. These days, instead of love-winds and baskets of corn, I see only frostbite and brown leaves in the gutters. I wake up anxious and early in November, even on holiday, as if my body has its own way of remembering those grief-filled Thanksgivings of recent years, and I can't help rewriting Lindsay's lines with bitter irony. *The fruition of best-laid plans. The end of love. Motherhood.*

In Wilkesboro that Thanksgiving morning, I had trouble finding the hospital and I worried that the wasted time could, in the end, worsen things for Emily, wondering how hard I would have to work to forgive myself should that time prove critical. Emily was leaning against her car door window and sobbing softly. I found it hard to take my eyes off her and watch the road. I could tell she thought the baby was already lost, and recalled how she'd mentioned the night before that it had been a while since she'd felt the baby's quickening, those subtle flutters of the second trimester.

When we finally arrived, I was surprised by the empty parking lots. I drove past the security guard on duty to the roundabout at the emergency entrance, where the ambulances unloaded their cargo and attendants stepped out for a bit of air and a smoke. An orderly standing nearby looked on, his expression softening when he saw

Emily's distress. She wouldn't meet his eyes and seemed to lack the strength to walk inside. He promptly fetched a wheelchair and guided us to the first examination room to find the admitting nurse, and left, clearly spooked. The emergency department seemed empty, too, implausibly so. I wondered if Thanksgiving was regarded as a slow time in medicine. Every nurse, orderly, and doctor we met that day seemed to have just awakened from a long nap.

Emily was despondent, already disappearing into grief. She told the nurse that she thought now maybe it'd been days since she felt the baby. She shed her clothes and waited on the examination bed.

"Are you cold?" I asked, offering to run out to the nurse's station for a blanket.

"Please don't leave." Her eyes told me there was nothing I could do, no way to solve this. I could only sit and wait.

A nurse entered briskly, but paused near the door, trying to catch my eye. I nodded. With a thick, toy-like syringe she drew a large sample of dark fluid from Emily's uterus.

"My baby. My poor baby," Emily cried.

"We don't know anything yet, dear," the nurse cut in. "This may just be a small, placental abruption. The doctors here can do amazing things."

I wrenched my eyes from the sight of the syringe, seizing on this new possibility. "Maybe it'll be okay. Remember what the birth coach said? No pregnancy is problem-free."

The quiet, almost surreptitious way the nurse filled the syringe with liquid reminded me of the way our obstetrician had efficiently and without our permission harvested the cord blood immediately after Virginia was born three years before. The group leader of our prenatal classes had warned us to specifically request that our baby be allowed to soak up every last bit of the cord blood before it was snipped, that it was particularly rich blood, full of nutrients vital to a newborn's early health, but in the rush, we had forgotten. Not for the last time had my daughter's presence struck me dumb.

Less than a minute after the nurse left with the syringe, the doctor entered the room looking as if he hadn't slept in days. An old-timer, he looked bloated and unhealthy. Broken capillaries webbed his cheeks and he had the broad nose of a heavy drinker. His shirt was stained on the sleeves and his pants had lost their crease below the knee. But he wore a genuinely warm smile, and I could tell Emily liked him immediately, even when he fumbled with the transducer, dropping it on her belly and causing her to flinch and clutch my forearm tighter. As Emily expected, the doctor couldn't find a heartbeat, and began asking her about the nature of the discharge she had experienced that morning—questions she couldn't answer.

He wheeled his stool over, sat down heavily, and lifted Emily's gown. As he began his examination, he seemed to fix his gaze on a particular quadrant of wall beyond Emily's left shoulder, high in the corner of the room. Instinctively, my eyes followed his line of sight to an abandoned spider web, visible only because of the dust that had accumulated on its strands and the cylindrical shell of a last meal suspended at its center.

"Ah, here it is. How far along were you?"

Neither one of us registered his change of verb tense.

"Twenty weeks," Emily whispered.

The doctor paused. "Well, this baby is much smaller than that," he said. "Don't worry, dear, this was not a 'mama' problem. This kind of thing is pretty common, but you shouldn't have any trouble trying again…when you're ready."

Clearly, he had intended to comfort us with those words, but I was still trying to make sense of his phrasing. *Not a mama problem.* What kind of problem then? Whose problem was it? He was telling us that the baby had stopped developing. But we were scheduled to find out the gender the following week, since the fetus had already proven clearly that it was my child by refusing at our last appointment to turn around and show us whether we were expecting a boy or a girl. We were in our fifth month. Our baby ought to have been able to hear, to make a fist. By twenty weeks, it should have had fingers and toes, eyelashes, even hair. It should have been flexing the muscles it had just developed.

"What would you like to do with it?" he asked, softly.

Was he lying to us, this kindly country doctor? Would it soften the blow somehow to think it was unavoidable, out of human hands, that nothing on this earth could have been done? If he was lying, did it mean all this might have been avoided? Could the baby have been saved had we not been so exhausted, driven, reckless? Women have healthy babies after working in fields, running marathons, pulling double shifts. I couldn't process his words, but Emily could. "We'd like to have a burial. Can we do that?"

"Of course." He turned to the nurse, who'd just returned to the room. "See if you can find a small jar in storage."

"Was it a boy or girl?" Emily asked.

"Oh, it wasn't developed enough to tell that. Like I said, this was not a 'mama' problem."

A few silent minutes later, the nurse handed me a pink pouch, explaining it had been knitted by a group of local widows for just this purpose. The pouch held a small glass jar with a stainless steel, screw-top lid. It looked like an old-fashioned canning jar. I must have looked incredulous because she quickly gave me, also, a little plastic pouch containing a simple gold cross, a small laminated sheet of helpful phone numbers, and a pamphlet on miscarriage and its aftermath of grief.

The next morning my mom's priest met us in the labyrinth beside the Episcopal Church. He led us in a prayer, then, after a ceremony of Biblical readings, a hymn I don't remember, and a prayer he intoned, we buried the jar with a small, plastic Winnie the Pooh and one of Virginia's toy cars. We also put into the grave Emily's wedding band. She'd asked me if I thought that was a good idea the night before. "It's a lovely idea. We can get new ones someday and I can give mine on a chain to Virginia when she's grown."

According to its website, the labyrinth at St. Paul's Coventry Chapel in Wilkesboro was created as a place to "quiet the mind, soothe the soul, and mend the heart. You walk the labyrinth by following the red brick path. To exit the labyrinth, reverse your path and walk back to the beginning and into your daily life once again." Before we exited into our daily life once more, Emily walked back and buried a sprig of berries from one of the bushes that line the outside wall. That night, Emily told me that as she knelt to place the pouch in the small grave I had dug, she tilted the jar and saw the sole of a foot surface out of the brown liquid. A perfect, pink foot. The fact that the following spring a new shrub seemed to have sprung from the very spot where we buried the baby wasn't quite enough to still the deep rage that this image of my child in the jar evokes in me to this day.

The following November, once again in Wilkesboro, having driven down from our new apartment in D.C., Emily and I delivered meals on Thanksgiving to shut-ins. Two years later, the year after Emily's own death, I made the trip again, but the soup kitchen staff was inundated with earnest, shiny faces, and simply didn't have enough jobs to go around. I sat in the hall for five hours monitoring the yellow trash barrels and watching an endless stream of young families and single, worn-down men sit to steaming meals on Styrofoam trays. Near the end of the day, I got a spot as dishwasher, but only in time to scrub exactly three pots. I stuck around long enough to drag those barrels to the dumpster one last time.

So much for my attempts to re-affix purpose and meaning to this shifty holiday, to recognize the enjoyment of abundance and gratitude in others even if I just wanted to drift through the hours as quickly as possible. I'd left my young daughter and son to celebrate with their grandparents, and I hadn't really done anything. Loneliness came upon me like a sickness. When my shift was through, I drove back to my parent's house with a growling stomach. The sun was setting behind the mountains, darkening everything. When I arrived, the house was silent. My parents had evidently fallen asleep while putting Langston down for his nap. Only Virginia was up, and I'd made it just in time to join her for a quiet supper of leftover sandwiches and pie.

And There Was Evening
and There Was Morning

For six days, I lay beside her in her bed.

For six days, the nurses and doctors whisked in and out, less and less frequently as time passed.

On the first day, when Emily relapsed into coma, Helen, the nurse with whom we had spent so much time, pleaded with me to move her from the ICU to a floor where they knew her, a unit more peaceful than this place where it seemed sirens answered each other in macabre counterpoint.

On the second day, Emily's mother asked to sit with her while I ate a meal. I declined.

On the third day, I helped the oncology nurses change the bedding. We rolled her groaning body on its side, minded the tubes of evacuation and hydration, pulled the old sheet from the corners and fitted on the new one, smoothing out the bunch against her back as much as we could, then rolled her onto her other side to pull the fresh sheet through.

On the fourth day, Emily's mother asked, again, to sit with her, and I agreed.

On the fifth day, I remembered a dream Emily had during her first hospital stay. In the dream the doctor who stood beside her bed was the devil in disguise. He waxed in a clinical yet cheerful way that she would not survive the night. She told me the next morning that, though she knew she was dreaming, she could not will herself to wake up. When I remembered the dream I left the bed to ask Helen if she thought today must be the day. During the night, green secretions from Emily's lungs had filled her oxygen mask. Helen changed the mask, cleaned her mouth and jaw, and said she didn't know, she didn't know.

On the seventh day, I allowed my parents to walk me from the always-darkness of the parking garage into winter sunlight, but not before I smashed the yellow call box with my fists, an act of echoing rage I took such pleasure in that it terrified my mother.

For six days, every decision seemed a concession, a failure of strength and faith and will. Bereft of everything else, I whispered the names of our children into her ear, and they were all I said to her of the world outside our curtained window.

On the seventh day, I arranged for her cremation, fast-tracking the death certificate so that we might hold the Funeral Mass before her body was burned.

On the ninth day, the funeral home furnished a casket so her body might be present at the chapel, as her father said it must.

That evening, I brought my children into my bed, sang my songs into their ears, and dreamed a dream that could not be.

PIGEONS AND TURTLEDOVES

THOUGHTS OF ETERNITY have always terrified me. Sometimes, at night, I try to trick myself into imagining the experience of never-endingness, and think myself into a cold sweat. My insides flip-flop and my breath catches in my throat. Usually, my first wife Emily had been able to sleepily talk me back down, but, sometimes, I would have to get up and move around a bit. Sitting at our shared desk, I'd try to read and write by the light of an industrial lamp Emily had picked up before we met. Surprisingly, the lamp cast a warm light, which I found comforting, especially on those nights when it illuminated the desolate and beautiful print that hung above the desk. The print had been a gift to her from her parents and every time I see it, I'm liable to fall into orbit, suspended by the mystery of its hold on me.

The print is a reproduction of a wood engraving by Fritz Eichenberg, his depiction of Saint Francis of Assisi's *Sermon to the Birds*. After my move to Mississippi, I hung it in my living room above the couch where its glass catches the late sun streaming through the blinds.

Eichenberg produced the engraving in 1964, which means he'd been contributing pro bono to Dorothy Day's *Catholic Worker* for more than a decade when he etched the image into existence. He is best known, perhaps, for his sensitive, interpretive illustrations for editions of classic literature, but his admiration for Day was great enough that, in addition to providing her lithographs for her magazine, he also illustrated her autobiography. A Jewish convert to Quakerism, Eichenberg presciently fled Nazi Germany before World War II. Like me, he attended the same high school as his first wife, but he and Mary were actual classmates, whereas I was a year behind Emily at Grimsley High School and we didn't meet until my last year of college. Also like me, Eichenberg lost his first wife to cancer after ten years of marriage. His wife Mary was thirty-six when she died, the same age as Emily had been at her death.

And as my own spiritual life turned out to be a restless one, so was his.

In an interview preserved by the Archives of American Art, Eichenberg explains that he "hit upon wood engraving as the best medium" because carving negative space into wood allowed him to "work from dark into light, or from black into white, with all the gradations—which is also symbolic procedure—a process which makes it possible for you to create life out of a void." A bit later in the conversation, he talks about his process:

> As you face the blank woodblock or the darkened
> surface of a lithographic stone, you create life out of
> it by throwing with your first touch of the graver—
> the first touch of your etching needle or razor blade.

Out of desolation, a little life—our eternal protest against annihilation. Looked at from a distance, the lithograph's composition resembles a keyhole with only the smallest light shining through from the other side of the door. In the right light, this impression is overwhelmingly evident.

Saint Francis stands at the scene's center, with his back to the viewer and his arms spread wide. His face is upturned at an almost impossible angle, but his posture is relaxed and his stance in contrapose. Birds surround him. Four perch on each arm, sixteen at his feet, and a halo of seven fly above his head. The range of species is impressive. There are large birds of prey, a rooster, a crane, and a raven. Two doves upstage an owl. There is as well a crow, a pheasant, and, startlingly, a vulture. Francis is thin but not frail. His feet are bare, and his hips, a walker's hips, are well-defined under the robe cinched at his waist by a rope. The robe is simple, his beard neatly trimmed. His eyes are closed. Though his brow is furrowed, his gesture and affect seem effortless, his body at peace, his face seemingly backlit by a shroud of blank canvas.

Before seeing the lithograph, I wasn't familiar with the story of Francis's sermon to the birds. The sermon, as it comes to us, was apparently written down by a member of his traveling band of followers, one of those young men who fell under his spell of asceticism and renunciation. An Italian monk, Brother Ugolino, first recorded "Sermon of the Birds" in the fourteenth century, as part of his "notabilia," that collected incidents in the life of the saint overlooked by official records. The legend is lengthy given the sermon's brevity, but charming. Here's the sermon is in its entirety.

> My little sisters, the birds, you ought to praise your Creator very much and always love him. He gave you feathers to clothe you, wings so that you can fly, and whatever else you needed. God made you noble among his creatures, and he gave you a home in the purity of the air. Though you neither sow nor reap, he nevertheless protects and governs you without any solicitude on your part.

What I knew of Francis didn't move me, particularly. His biography reveals him as the favored son of a rich father, who enjoys an ideal adolescence of wealth and popularity. Born Giovanni di Bernadorne in 1181, he founded the Franciscan Order in 1209, and his spiritual conversion took place after he was wounded and captured in a battle between Assisi and Perugia. He spent a year or so as prisoner of war until his father paid his ransom. He returned a changed man, renouncing his father's wealth to begin life again as a wandering preacher and animal lover. It smacks of the privilege of guilt, which makes his adoption by 20th century ecologists a bit predictable.

After his wife's death, Eichenberg's work increasingly reflects religious subjects. Though he tended to dismiss the aesthetic qualities of his *Catholic Worker* illustrations in interviews, his work with Day, which began in the early 1950s, succeeded in bringing together both his spiritual interests and his ongoing sensitivity to questions of social justice. Such questions were undoubtedly fueled by political convictions that had, in all likelihood, saved his life two decades before. In 1933, against the advice of everyone he knew in Germany, he emigrated to the United States with his small family.

Before *The Long Loneliness* became the title of Dorothy Day's autobiography, it was the title of another of Eichenberg's wood engravings. This one is housed in the Guilford College Art Gallery in my hometown of Greensboro, North Carolina. A reproduction of the print, created in 1952, hangs in my in-laws' house, in what was once Emily's bedroom. Mary sits, soul-pierced, on the left side of the print, holding her globe-like belly with both hands. Her face is drawn with pain, and her eyes, like the Saint's, are closed. Clearly, she is experiencing the pangs of labor. Hovering at her left shoulder, an angel bends to whisper in her ear, a gentle and apprehensive birth coach. Together, their bodies form a frame within a frame, but they seem to frame nothingness, the great emptiness of the scene. The rest of the lithograph is packed with symbolic depiction. Opposite the angel, a road in the foreground winds its way inexorably toward three small crosses on a distant hill. In the upper right corner, Eichenberg has shaped the blank wood into a dove.

Eichenberg's Mary looks older than the Mary of the Gospels. Perhaps he had been thinking of his late spouse, who was named for her. After Eichenberg's Mary died, it's said he turned away from the Quakerism of his childhood and toward eastern religions. While he admired Day and followed her pure brand of Catholicism for years, he never, apparently, seriously considered the faith a source of solace. I understood completely. Emily's return to Catholicism occurred before we met, during the long loneliness of her time as a single adult in D.C.

Though I considered myself a spiritual person, it was the intellectual complications of maintaining a contemporary life of faith that most interested me about Emily's discipline. Religion reinforced rather than relieved my terror of eternity. Of course, I was equally troubled by the prospect of non-existence, so I was a proper Existentialist. Emily was untroubled by both potentialities, which befuddled me. This difference of ours was larger than perhaps we realized and marked me, I think, as younger than the one year between us. For Eichenberg, the woodcut aims at synthesis, a solemn evocation of private and public sacrifice, which makes me think again of the work of my own first wife, Emily, and her book on the near sacrifice of Isaac and its history of interpretation.

One morning, near the end of Emily's first hospital stay, I promised her I would convert to Catholicism. This sudden decision was consistent with my religious biography. I have suffered through baptismal ritual four times. Growing up, my family moved from Quaker to Presbyterian, Baptist to Moravian. Every time we joined a new congregation, I experienced a rush of conviction and strode down to the font to reenact my rebirth in whatever faith had flushed my face and swelled my racing heart. When I returned to the pew, my family kindly hid their smiles. My parents finally settled on the Episcopal Church, but I was in college then, so remained unclaimed, vacillating between the tenets of my childhood and unbelief, steadied only occasionally by guilt.

The priest who'd married us had come to town to see Emily and performed a family mass in her hospital room, when I blurted out my promise. Emily was gaining strength by the hour, it seemed, her numbers improving with every panel of blood work. The antibiotics were working, and she'd begun moving around a bit, sitting for an hour or so in the recliner I'd been calling my bed for almost a week. On occasion, I was able to bring Langston with me. At one point, we overheard some of the nurses referring to Emily's going home day, though the doctors hadn't yet fixed a date. That was almost nine years ago, and though Langston has since been christened and the two children and I attend mass sometimes, I've yet to take a single formal step to become Catholic.

I am not sure I can articulate why I haven't converted, but I'm certain my reticence has something to do with those terrors of my nights, which have since merged with two experiences I had during the summer and fall of Emily's illness. I'd call them *spiritual*, I suppose, though thinking back, I'm filled not with consolation but with self-doubt and despair. How common each episode now seems, however singular they felt at the time.

The first experience took place during the rush and rattle that succeeded diagnosis. Before Emily was to begin treatment, a medi-port was inserted into her chest to prevent her veins from blowing out from use, which might delay treatment. The operation initially seemed routine but ended up lasting twice as long as we'd been told. In the waiting room, I watched the minutes tick by, unable even to decipher the words of the book on my lap, trying to fight the rising feeling that something was wrong. Just as my hysteria was becoming physiological, my body suddenly relaxed. I felt I was becoming a part of my surroundings. The cool plastic of the chair's arm became my own, the hard wall behind my head received me as easily as if it were a soft, pliant pillow. I sensed Emily beside me. I smelled her, felt her warmth, and I lost track of time.

When the surgeon finally appeared to give me his report, I felt sure he was there to tell me something had gone wrong, that Emily had died. Had this all been my mind protecting itself, reassuring the other part of me that refused to admit she might be dying? "Sometimes these things take longer than we think. She should be waking up soon," the surgeon said. My relief overwhelmed me and I found myself embracing him.

Over the years, when I've reflected on this incident, part of me has wanted it to have happened the way I felt sure it was happening. Had Emily died that day, I might console myself and my children that their mother was still near, somewhere out there, that it was only our clumsy way of experiencing the world that prevented us from knowing her. She might be right beside us at any moment, only vibrating at a different pitch, singing a song in a voice too high for our poor ears to hear. This incident wasn't the last time I found I couldn't trust myself, my apprehension of the reality that surrounded me, the wishes of my own mind. I caught my wife's scent, despite the disinfectant that saturated the room. I felt her warmth, though she was five air-conditioned rooms and a busy hallway away.

A month and a half later, I heard phantom voices above the quiet hum of Emily's hospital room. It was early afternoon, and I had about an hour before I had to pick up Virginia from school. Emily was asleep on her side, facing me, as I sat beside her. Suddenly, I heard singing, a music of sounds, and though unintelligible, as consoling as a children's choir. At first, I looked to the hallway, but our door was shut, as was our one window. It had been an ordinary Wednesday. The team of doctors and students had been by after lunch and, as usual, were cautiously encouraging. The antibiotics, as always, had had their desired effect, and it was hoped that Emily might be able to go home the first of the week. No one knew (how could they?) that in a couple of days her kidneys would begin to fail and that she would lapse into a catatonic state. No one knew that this stay, our second since she began chemotherapy, would be our longest.

But as I said, it was an ordinary day. I'd been reading a new biography of Shakespeare, one that claimed his works were written in a kind of code, that he'd been a cautious activist attempting to console and cheer English Catholics under the reigns of Elizabeth and James. Emily and I were alone in the room, but now there was this unexplainable sound, an alien singing. Something was suddenly there with me, rocking my soul. *Let her hear this, too*, I prayed. *Let her hear only this, now and forever in this place. Spare her the brisk, cheery voices of the staff. Let her fall deaf to the hum and buzz of the machines, the caws of the monitors. Let her be deaf to groans and gossip, the shuffling of slippers on the polished floor, the rattle of I.V. stands, the flushes and the roll of beds.*

Does Eichenberg's Mary trust the angel whispering in her ear? The angel's mouth is hidden behind her hand, and whatever she is saying, it is for Mary's ears only. Our senses confuse us, and they're our only way of knowing the world. I tell my students this confusion is essential to an authentic experience of beauty, but when I perceive ambiguities, they tend to bring about confusion that drives me to try to see the cause, the why, even if it brings fresh pain. Conversely, Emily delighted in ambiguity, which most often had inspired her to return to her work with renewed vigor. I envied her this and often wondered which of our muses was more fundamental to our human existence: hers of uncertainty or mine of guilt. In the months after Emily's death,

I'd go back to her study of the *akedah*. When I woke myself up with grief or doubt, I'd fish out Emily's manuscript from underneath all of the detritus of my day-to-day life, all the cough drop wrappers, baby rattles, tissues, and shopping lists that had accumulated in the deep drawer of my bedside table. I confess I was rarely enlightened.

One of the challenges articulated by Emily in the first chapter of her book, *Demanding Our Attention*, and which proves to be a catalyst for the original thrust of her argument is, as she writes, "the problem of relating to an ancient and strange text as a 21st century person." She questions how "a text produced in (and producing) a world so removed from our own be a crucial source for how we are to act and to be now?" Precisely. Emily's interests were far-ranging, and to answer this question she relied on contemporary cultural and literary critiques as well as exegesis of Biblical narrative, moving from analysis to original theory. At the book's conclusion, she claims these difficult approaches "are our means of performing actions necessary to be in relationship with God and others." Emily's desire for and belief in synthesis, to draw and sustain connections despite deep divides of discipline and convention, is everywhere in the book.

At the end of her reading of Kierkegaard's *Fear and Trembling*, Emily writes that "the labor of reading the *akedah* is an ongoing (and repeated) act, best undertaken when we are 'laden' with the awfulness of taking the story seriously, as we try to walk up the mountain with Abraham and Isaac." We are additionally burdened, she says, by the recognition that our reading of this story will never satisfy us. Indeed, our failures may "lead us deeper into self-doubt." It is a labor, like the process of grief without hope of resolution.

In the final chapter, she argues that critical engagement "presupposes that there is something there, a text, a person...that is other than us, prior to and beyond what we make of it." She notes in her own reading of Genesis 22 "that God appears to be the sole and possibly arbitrary force against the fulfillment of the promise," which is part of what makes this narrative unique among the Biblical narratives of promise and reward. She claims that the *akedah* "suggests a deeper complication" in the relationship between God and Abraham than one simply based on promise, obedience, and reward.

Near the end of her book, Emily focuses on the unresolvable ambiguity of this sparse narrative, focusing finally on the ambiguities surrounding Isaac, "whose very existence is orchestrated by God outside the natural course of events." She notes "the long tradition, evident in ancient midrash, of viewing the story as a trial for Isaac as much as for Abraham." Isaac and Abraham. Trials of confusion and guilt, tales of doubt and dismay.

But Isaac is spared, the promise fulfilled. What happens when the story is of despair rather than dismay? To whom could someone like me relate in the story? In those months after Emily's death, eternity and oblivion both seemed, more than ever, like cruel fates. Now, I find myself rereading her book not for wisdom or clarity, but to hear the echo of that voice that for most of my adult life was both spur and consolation.

The Biblical story that stands most directly behind Eichenberg's *The Long Loneliness* is Chapter 2 of Luke, not 22 of Genesis. Mary and Joseph bring an infant Jesus to Jerusalem to present him to the Lord and to offer a sacrifice according to what is said in the law of the Lord, "a pair of turtledoves, or two young pigeons," where they meet Simeon, the righteous and devout. The Holy Spirit was upon him, and, so inspired, he tells new mother Mary that

> Behold, this child is set for the fall and rising of many
> in Israel, and for a sign that is spoken against (and a
> sword will pierce through your own soul also), that
> thoughts out of many hearts may be revealed.

It sounds like hell. I am still grateful that many of my thoughts of that year of Emily's death have never been revealed. How often did my wishes turn to curses? How often did my desires diminish to base need?

Following this chapter and verse, the gospel introduces Anna, a prophetess, who was "of a great age, having lived with her husband seven years from her virginity, and as a widow till she was eighty four...And coming up at that very hour she gave thanks to God, and spoke of him to all who were looking for the redemption of Jerusalem." Despite her age and litany of hardships, she kept her senses all her life. They did not fail her, as they failed me, as they continue to fail me, and as they must have failed Isaac.

The birds of Eichenberg's *Sermon to the Birds* are needful. They look like pets impatient for a treat, but all Francis has to offer them is words. His face is upturned, also, as if he expects to be fed, too. It seems that he is one of them, the harried mama-bird of some nursery rhyme, whose assumed calm is really wise madness, his loose sleeves pulled by gravity into thin wings. What words is *he* hearing? Why does he trust them so? Some of the explications of this story claim that the birds, when they left Francis, spread his sermon throughout the world, each in its own language. What if a bird dropped out of the sky tomorrow to speak to us? Who among us would trust our senses?

In an autobiographical turn of the concluding pages of Emily's final chapter, she confesses that her long engagement with Genesis 22 has already changed her conviction, assumptions, and actions of her moral self. In the end, her conviction that the "nature of this interpretive 'moment'...and the experience of reading itself demand scrutiny" fuels and informs the book. For my part, I can't help reading and re-reading into Eichenberg's prints. In fact, my thinking has begun to conflate the two distinct narratives behind his works.

Lately, I've begun to see Saint Francis of Assisi as another Mary, not the adult Jesus with whom tradition has tried to link him. He's one of the birds, perhaps listening to another angel singing in his ear, who's invisible because of the brightness of divine light. The Saint's senses have failed him; his eyes are closed. But he's concentrating. He is trying, impossibly, to comprehend every word.

Whispers of Gratitude and Praise

Eight and a half years ago, the first ambitious task I undertook after I moved from Washington, D.C. to my North Carolina apartment was to write letters to family and friends who'd been so helpful during my wife Emily's illness and death. It took me six months. Toward the end of this undertaking, I hired a young woman to look after Langston, our then six-month-old, for two mornings a week. I selected stationary of hummingbirds and dragonflies. I tried my best to write neatly. I sat in the same antique swivel writing chair in which I sit now, a graduation gift from Emily's parents, and made and checked my list twice, though I'm sure I left people out.

Part of the reason I wrote these letters was because of Emily's minor but persistent fear that she hadn't sent thank-you notes to everyone who'd given us wedding gifts. We'd divided the responsibility along family lines, but then we moved and, three months later, moved again. Somewhere along the way, the list had been lost. Even after ten years of marriage, she'd felt mortified when she thought about it. So, in the first six months after her death, I wrote and mailed eighty or so letters. The job seemed beyond me, though I went at it as dutifully as a Deep South bride.

Three and a half years later, after yet another move, one of my new colleagues at Delta State University told me the story of a young woman who suddenly dropped his Shakespeare class late in the semester. She was smart and capable, and had engaged honestly in the course, and my colleague was fond of her. *Why?* he asked. *Why must you quit now? Your grades have been exemplary.* She told him she had gotten married that summer and now had over five hundred thank-you notes to write—Shakespeare had to go. Decades later, the situation still exasperated him and my sympathy for her surprised him.

The business of grief is pure prose. Give this poor subject a verb, keep it busy. Or get it going again, so it might progress along its sentence. Poetry was lost to me. Its concentration, its formalities rebuffed and appalled. I wanted straight report, and people obliged me. In the first year after Emily's death, I received dozens of books on grief and mourning. I couldn't read them all, but kept them anyway. Even now, I'll come upon one while scanning a shelf and my mind will snap back to the time I received it. Time travel of a sort: for an instant, I am completely there, returning to the smells, discomforts, and the old tugging hollowness in my belly of those moments. This gravity of grief still pulls at me, as if I might swallow myself.

The body of contemporary English language literature on mourning seemed to me then impressively large, and I still lack the heart to delve into why we are drawn so enthusiastically to these litanies of bereavement, to grief and its eventual, necessary sublimation. I wondered why I hadn't really noticed them before, these long, lonely cries of anguish.

Unsurprisingly, Joan Didion's *The Year of Magical Thinking* was among the first books I received. I wanted to like the book, to need it, but individual words and phrases kept getting in the way: *Corvette, New York, Richard Carroll in Beverly Hills, Brooks Brothers shorts, Quintana was at Barnard, Forty years, December 30*. Why should their wealth and length of time together matter? Grief is grief, but I envied her the years, the certainty of her vocation, the seemingly gentle existence. I envied her the adulthood of her child. Emily had died on the first of December, two and a half months shy of her thirty-seventh birthday, when our oldest child was five and a half years, our youngest five months old. I even envied Didion those twenty-nine days of December. It didn't matter that on December 30, 2004, when Didion's husband John Gregory Dunne suffered a fatal heart attack as they sat down to supper, Emily and I had celebrated Virginia's third Christmas in our two-bedroom 1908 bungalow, whose disproportionately large hall and high ceilings made a perfect court for the Nerf basketball hoop

WHISPERS OF GRATITUDE AND PRAISE

our daughter received as a gift. I felt like being unfair, being cruel. *Privilege, privilege, privilege, privilege*, echoed in my head, like some lost line of *Lear*. I raged that Emily was denied the satisfaction of a full working life, the anxiety and pleasure of watching her daughter and son reach out for their own adulthoods. And I put the book down.

Five years later, I picked the book up again, but something still nagged at me. What bothered me wasn't Didion's life of privilege but her presumption of the reader's empathy. Beneath her retelling of the series of tragedies, beyond the alternation of restraint and confession, there lies presumption, which seems rooted in the certainty of her status as an important writer. I didn't see her flaws as resonant and meaningful, I couldn't interpret, couldn't translate, couldn't read into her story what she doesn't say, and I didn't cherish the sense of alienness I felt from seeing the difference between her life and mine.

I was thirty-five, midway through a life I wanted over, when I told Virginia that her mother was dead. We were sitting together on the flight of cement steps that led up to the ball field across the street from our apartment. Saturdays that first fall in D.C., the three of us, Virginia, her mother, and I, woke to the shouts and cheers of a dozen teams playing youth soccer on portable goals. The field was empty now, though the weather wasn't yet bitter. My daughter and I had taken a walk together as soon as I got home from the hospital. We didn't go far, just looped around her school, passing the two ornamental trees, now bare, on each side of the school's front steps. Before Emily became sick, when it seemed I had nothing but time, I used to amuse Virginia and her classmates by climbing those trees then taking pratfalls in the sandy ground. The sight of the trees almost brought me to tears, so we cut across the ball field to end up where we began.

I hadn't seen either of my children for almost a week, not since the evening Emily had relapsed into a hepatic coma and I'd been forced to concede that her life was ending. I'd intended to break the news to Virginia gently, a mere whisper, while holding her in my arms, but as it turned out, I ruined it. I blurted out the words. It was the third time that day I had to acknowledge my wife's death out loud.

I'd spent the last three days beside Emily in the hospital bed in the ICU whispering my steady stream of gratitude and praise, convinced she could still hear me. I'd thanked her for the gift of Virginia and Langston, for taking direction of our lives, for getting me where I needed to be as husband, father, and man.

At some point during the previous night, Emily's father suggested I reassure her that it was okay to stop fighting, that it was all right for her to let go. I tried to do that, but couldn't. I kept giving her outs, caveats, as if defiance were still possible, as if the end to the story might even then be rewritten. That morning around nine, I gave in to sleep. I dreamed I pulled a white rabbit by the neck out of a top hat, and woke minutes later to find her cheek already cold.

God help me, I still thought something might be done, if only I moved fast enough. I pushed the button for Helen, the veteran nurse. Six days earlier, she'd intervened to have Emily moved from the ICU so we might have the solitude of a single room the time left to us. Helen didn't come right away, evidently thinking that I'd called her to witness the time on the death certificate and begin whatever preparations were needed. In my confusion, I was dumbfounded by her lack of urgency. To keep from shouting, I called home and told my mother Emily was gone.

While I waited for my parents and Emily's to arrive, I told Helen about having briefly fallen asleep and woken to find Emily had died. "That's common," she said. "Sometimes, they wait for you to step out of the room, especially if they think you can't handle it."

Her matter-of-fact tone reminded me of a conversation I'd had with a healthcare worker two months before. This was during Emily's longest hospital stay. She'd been declared a fall risk and staff had been assigned to stay nights to help her when needed. One night, late, while Emily slept, I asked the woman how long she had been doing this kind of work.

"Three years," she replied without glancing up. She was in her fifties, probably, and had spent her entire shift reading a romance novel, one of those flimsy mass markets with the salacious cover that Emily and I used to sell so many of when we worked at the bookstore.

"It must be hard," I said, meaning emotionally exhausting, but she misunderstood.

"Yeah. But you learn what to look for. I can tell when they're close, so I start getting them ready, cleaning them up and changing their clothes." My eyes darted to the bed and I said a silent prayer of gratitude that Emily was still asleep. The image of this woman pushing and prodding people in their last moments of life as if they were petulant toddlers was the last of our conversation.

Fond as I was of Helen, I was angry at her for how easily she fell into routine, and I was glad when she left the room. Was it the pressure from the breathing mask that had turned the corners of Emily's mouth up into a slight smile? As I washed her face, I saw, suddenly, how completely the disease had ravaged her body. Bilirubin had turned her skin and hair burnt orange. Her body, swollen from I.V. fluid, was distorted, yet she still seemed impossibly small. My mind raged. The part of my mind that never knows when to shut itself down couldn't see my love of the past twelve years, and instead conjured one of those unfortunate Iron Age specimens exhumed from a bog. Her skin was pocked in places and filled with fluids, while her cheeks were hollow and her lips were thin and cracked. The realization hit me: My wife was dead.

Now, on the cement steps across from our apartment, I held Virginia to me, feeling the warmth of her sobbing body through our coats and looking across the field at her two-story, brick schoolhouse. That August, on Virginia's first day of kindergarten, I'd taken a photograph of her to show Emily. In the shot, Virginia's hands are clasped in front of her as if she were a care-worn grandmother, not a five-year-old excited for the start of another school year. She's leaning forward, head inclined toward the camera, worried that I'm going to mess it up. One of the ornamental trees is behind her. Her mother is in the hospital for the first time since the diagnosis. A blood infection, which we will learn originated in her infusion port, will throw off the schedule of chemo. Our one-month-old son, Langston, is being shown the flowers in the neighbor's window box by his grandmother. The days are very warm and it's still light out when Virginia goes to sleep.

It's her first day of kindergarten and not one of us can yet imagine the things we will have to say to each other.

Virginia eventually stopped sobbing but kept her face pressed against my chest. As gently as I was able, I scooped her up, keeping her wrapped in the folds of my coat. She was so quiet I thought she might fall asleep the way she used to as a toddler after a tantrum. Holding her to me, I walked to the apartment to join Langston and the rest of our family and begin the hard work of mourning.

One of the complications of Emily's cancer was the edema in her torso, which gave her the appearance of being pregnant long after Langston's induction. I rarely noticed. Eventually, though, fluid crossed the lung wall and compromised her breathing. The procedure to insert a catheter to drain her lungs was one of the simpler operations she had to endure. The surgeon was straightforward with Emily: "I mostly deal with lung patients and can tell them with some certainty that they will dry up soon. It may take you longer. I just don't know."

A home nurse taught me how to drain and dispose of the fluid pouches, how to change the dressing on her IV, and administer the antibiotics Emily seemed to continually need. This was done so that Emily might spend more time at home. The woman, who was kind and patient, spent hours in our apartment going over details while Emily napped. After the nurse left, I joined Emily in bed. "Sorry that took so long. She was very sweet and showed me everything twice. Very friendly."

"Well, of course," was Emily's response. "She took one look at me and knew you'd be available soon."

The exercise we'd once done together, our private time, was replaced by this home care. Somehow, we kept the procedure hidden from Virginia. When the time came, I would put Langston in his crib, plug Virginia into Colin Firth's version of *Pride and Prejudice* (still one of her favorites), and watch as the clear bag filled with fluid. The practice almost broke me every time, but the knowledge that I had mere moments to complete the draining kept me focused. Emily took the most invasive and mortifying procedures with infinite patience and equanimity. Her trust in her doctors never wavered. Perhaps she knew there was nothing they could do beyond attending to her comfort. Perhaps she knew that she was moving, inexorably, beyond their help or harm.

I wouldn't let her talk about death, her death. Part of the reason cancer produces such fear, and such hope, is its capriciousness. In the face of the overwhelming evidence of her deteriorating body, I offered up exception after exception. Small victories indicated great progress. Setbacks were to be expected and necessary to any recovery. For the most part, Emily put herself completely in my hands. Despite how irrevocably our old life had vanished, we almost never squabbled. Our only argument those four months occurred over mayonnaise. She'd just been discharged and craved a turkey sandwich. I wanted her to lay off the mayo. "We need to shock your body into health," I preached. Her oncologist settled things at our next visit, and simply said, "Emily should eat whatever she wants."

In fact, once the hospital stays began, Emily and I spent most of our time together in silence, holding hands, lying in her hospital bed. After diagnosis, she never cried. She worked toward health the same way she approached everything in her life: patiently, doggedly, giving the present moment its full significance without forgetting for a second what it all meant—why we had to keep trying. Yet at the same time, she turned increasingly inward, which gave the impression she was at peace. Late one night, while I was catching up on grading, she joined me on the couch. "How did I get cancer?" she asked, as she leaned her head on my shoulder. She didn't expect me to answer.

She had no family history of the disease. There was only the pregnancy. I remember reading somewhere that for women who have their first child after thirty, one in three thousand will develop breast cancer during a subsequent pregnancy. Emily was thirty-one when Virginia was born. It now sounds like a sports statistic to me, overly specific and yet with such a range as to be almost meaningless.

Time with the kids grew increasingly shorter. Emily was exhausted from the chemotherapy, the antibiotics, and the cancer itself. Every afternoon at three, she roused herself to hear about Virginia's day at school, and she loved having Langston in bed with her. She was afraid she would fall asleep while I was out of the room, so we ordered a co-sleeper that attached directly to the bed. Langston's godmother, Lahra, would stop by after work to sit with Emily and the baby while Virginia and I prepared supper. Lahra and Emily had met the year before at new faculty orientation and quickly became friends. Quick intimacy was one of Emily's most endearing gifts, and I wondered if Emily might have found it easier to talk with Lahra, in order to spare us her sadness. "She just wants to listen to my day," Lahra told me when I asked. I still don't know if Emily was seeing what I wouldn't allow myself, or anyone else to see. She must have known I needed the carrot of hope to keep going.

But I also had anger. My anger burned efficiently, fueled me through my nights and days. I spent much of that fall in transit, getting to or from the hospital, my classes, the medical supply store, the pharmacy, or the grocery store for the organic fruits and vegetables I was forcing down our throats. I learned the city better in those weeks than I had during the year and a half before. I no longer walked to class or the store; I couldn't spare the time. When I slept, I no longer dreamed. I caught a cold that wouldn't go away, so I wore a mask when I was at the hospital, rising with the early morning vitals check to run home and see Virginia off to school. I'd greet whoever had stayed with the kids that night—friend or parent or grandparent—and greet the sitter who would spend the morning with Langston while I raced to class. I taught on auto-pilot. I lived on auto-pilot. There was always somewhere I had to be. Arrive at the hospital by noon. Pick up Virginia at 3:15. Sing Langston to sleep. Read to Virginia. Return to the hospital by nine. I needed the anger, needed it to persist, to feed upon itself, to go nuclear in order not to cool into despair, despite the fact that I couldn't always keep it under control. In truth, I looked for opportunities to let it out.

Once, on the way home from Langston's two-month-old vaccinations, a man made the mistake of shouting at me when I cut him off in traffic. I chased him down. When he pulled over and got out of the car yelling, I charged at him. My mom was with me and, faintly, I heard her shouting. "Please. His wife's very sick."

The man, bless him, tried to reason with me. "Look. You pulled out in front of me. What was I supposed to do?"

I picked a spot on his face. Like a camera, my eye focused on a freckle on his left cheek. I was an instant from hitting him and I was exhilarated. Something in my expression must have told him that I wanted this and that I would not stop. He got in his car and screeched away. When I returned to my car, I saw Langston asleep in the backseat. He'd kicked off his blanket and I was brought up short by the blood-dotted Band-Aids on his thighs.

Near the end of October, things appeared, finally, to look up. Emily had been home almost a week after the month-long hospital stay. Though a stubborn cold still nagged me, Emily was feeling stronger than she had in weeks. She was eating better, and her oncologist was so encouraged that she had even allowed her to resume her chemo regimen. In fact, when Dr. Liu reported the results of Emily's latest labs, taken on our first visit to the office after discharge, she hugged her. Emily had received her second dose of chemotherapy before she left the hospital, and if her condition continued to improve, she would have the third between Halloween and Thanksgiving.

We were looking forward to Halloween. Virginia had decided to dress up as Glinda the Good Witch and Emily had ordered the costume, which came with a ridiculously blond wig. While I roamed the neighborhood trick-or-treating with Virginia, Emily planned on watching from the steps of our apartment building, Langston beside her, asleep on a blanket.

It was not to be. Halloween morning, Emily woke feeling weak, experiencing tremors in her arms and legs. Another infection, I thought. She had to be admitted immediately. When I arrived the next morning to share the pictures I'd taken of our trick-or-treating, the nurse refused to let me near Emily until I'd seen a doctor myself. I couldn't stop coughing and was sweating through my clothes. Immediately, I went to the nearest walk-in clinic and learned I had pneumonia. The doctor who saw me said I could avoid being admitted to the hospital myself if I promised him I would get some rest. "Please try," he said, and wrote out scripts for a heavy course of antibiotics and a codeine-laced cough syrup. When I returned to the hospital, Emily was sleeping. The nurse told me it was, indeed, another infection. Emily would probably have to be there for a week, provided no additional complications came up. I curled up in the blue chair beside her bed and held her hand as I grieved for the Halloween night we'd planned and the codeine charmed me to a dreamless sleep.

Why were the quiet moments of those four months the first to fade from my memory? Because I know there were pleasures, even during this time. Invariably though, they were characterized by stillness. Suddenly, we had nowhere to be, no doctor to see or be seen by, no medicine to fetch or administer, no supper to whip up, no child to sing to sleep, no class to teach. Often, early on, Emily and I would walk. The only important thing was that we not name a landing-place. We'd walk aimlessly the blocks of our neighborhood, pushing Langston in his stroller and watching Virginia skip ahead. In the hospital, Emily and I would walk the floors, discover nooks like the warm hallway of glass on the high floor (was it the sixth?) that overlooked the leafy inner courtyard, the sunlight there so present it warmed even the floor. Emily felt the warmth through her blue slippers and it so delighted her that she made me take off my shoes to feel it too. By unspoken agreement, we did not name this miraculous spot as our destination on subsequent walks, but we always ended up here, shoeless and smiling.

A week after Halloween, I gave myself a black eye. Langston had a bad night, and we'd fallen asleep together in my armchair after his 3 a.m. feeding. The following morning, after dropping Virginia at school and seeing Langston off on his morning walk with the sitter from Georgetown, I had a half hour to get to class. I couldn't keep my eyes open, couldn't string a sentence together even after a cold shower, and so I gave myself a little slap on the cheek as I stood at the mirror, shaving. Then I slapped myself again. Though I was alone in the apartment, I closed the bathroom door. The slaps became punches until the pain woke me to my life.

At the playground that afternoon, I told the mother of one of Virginia's friends that I'd run into one of our heavy wooden benches while giving Virginia a ride on my back around the living room. Why wouldn't she believe it? I'd spent half my waking hours the last five years playing horse and super-villain, hibernating bear, pirate king, and hopping bandit, prop and foil to whatever games Virginia and her friends dreamed up. Emily had given me this privilege; her gig paid the big bills. She worked hard at her job, cared deeply about teaching, cared even for the other obligations that accompany a college teaching position in a way I didn't quite understand. And I marveled at her unflagging energy and unwavering attention. When at home, she was completely at home—completely with me and with Virginia. Before the move to D.C., I taught nights, and so we traded off caring for Virginia during the week. When Emily came home at five, I left to prep and teach, knowing I would find the evidence of their activities on my return: chalk drawings on the walk outside, the scent of bubble bath in the bathroom, a fresh watercolor painting hung up to dry over the mantle.

I couldn't have been the parent she was, the parent she so desperately wanted to be to both our children. I wouldn't have had the strength to fight for my life the way she did those four months. After her death, a dear family friend wrote that "Emily seemed to have the inside scoop on everything." Yes, I thought, because she always found the center of her world, always at home in her life. Her daughter, I see now, will have something of her mother's mixture of enthusiasm and grace, a seemingly limitless capacity for anticipating and enjoying new experiences and the rich gift of empathy.

When Emily was with you, she was with you wholly. I both admired and envied this in her and I almost always failed to appreciate it properly. Now, I look for reminders of it in the people I meet, and I warm to strangers immediately when I see a glimpse of Emily's character in a glance or sigh. As this has often proved mortifying to me and unsettling to them, I've come to view it as easy penance for taking for granted the real thing, though I held it in my arms for twelve years. Emily wouldn't have been so childish as to give herself a black eye or terrify a commuter trying only to make it home after work. She wouldn't have needed anger to do what must be done. Often, that fall, I realized how patient she was with me, allowing me to bungle the things I tried to do for her without a whisper of caution or complaint.

I had to put down Joan Didion's book, but eventually I picked up others. The spring after Emily died, I mailed off the last of my letters and took myself to lunch at a Jamaican restaurant. The place was beside a used bookstore, so I went there next. I still wasn't much interested in resuming my bookish life, but this day I picked up an anthology of "death poems" in the Japanese tradition, compiled and edited by Yoel Hoffman. In his lengthy introduction to the poems, Hoffman notes, "[i]n haiku, there is an attempt to 'say something without saying it.' That which remains unsaid tells more than the words and yet is unclear without them." But the tradition of Japanese death poems predates the tradition of haiku.

The anthology also includes the death poems of Zen monks and Samurai. Because "[m]ost samurai of the time lived and died by the sword," it was customary for defeated warriors to be permitted time to say their death poems before execution or suicide. So ingrained was this tradition that the custom of warriors composing death poems survived into the 20th century. As Hoffman tells us, during World War II, "the youth who died in suicide units often left death poems, as did most officers of the Japanese army."

The first Zen poet anthologized in the book "died on the twentieth day of the second month 1387." Though I knew this date referred to the lunar calendar, not the Gregorian, I nevertheless took this as a sign— Emily had been born on the twentieth of February. Here is the poem:

> Look straight ahead. What's there?
> If you see it as it is
> You will never err.

The poet's name was Bessui Tokesho, and he wrote long before the haiku tradition began in Japan. Included in the anthology are three poets who died on the twentieth day of the second month, and three different poets who died at the age of thirty-six, the same age Emily was at her death. Here's one by a poet named Geki, who died in 1927.

> One spot, alone,
> Left glowing in the dark:
> My snotty nose.

Hoffman tells us that Geki "prefaced his poem with the words 'laughing at myself'" before committing suicide. I was happy my letter-writing was behind me, but my bitterness still shadowed me. Briefly, I wished I'd written Geki's poem.

Because I'd refused to discuss even the possibility of her death, I was forced to rely on my memory of a conversation we'd had after her grandmother died years before. Emily's mother had sent her some of her grandmother's ashes and we'd been debating whether to keep them or find a pretty spot to scatter them.

"We should all be cremated," Emily said.

"I don't know," I said. "It's too sterile or something. And the thought of being scattered to the four winds creeps me out."

"Better than being locked in a box."

The exchange would serve to guide me as I sleepwalked through the industry of her funeral.

Her colleagues at Georgetown arranged for a mass to be held at Dahlgren Chapel, the oldest chapel on the campus. The priest who'd married us and christened Virginia, and who would, in time, christen Langston, presided over the service. The number of people from every phase of Emily's life who'd come on such short notice stunned me. Many had flown or driven through the night. Emily's father and I spoke. At first, I'd resisted. Her death still felt more theoretical than real. Her death felt like my death or the deaths of my children. I felt participating in the ceremony would somehow make me culpable, as if my utterance would force me to more fully acknowledge the world without her. In the end, the shame I'd no doubt one day feel at my inability to say something meaningful about Emily in front of her family and friends forced me to the ambo. In my remarks, I said something about the fierce, arrogant pride I felt at being her husband.

Perhaps, as grief has no depth or breadth, and seems limitless, we ought to approach mourning—our ritual reaction to grief—without a destination in mind, without wanting it to get better, without wanting to move beyond it. We may as well ask to move beyond ourselves. Perhaps the desire to move beyond mourning is just the death wish itself disguised, the wish to journey to the beloved, not bring her back.

From my office chair, I can just see into the bedroom closet. On the top shelf, alongside the boxes of papers and photos and jewelry and keepsakes, Emily's ashes wait inside their urn. I'd planned on spreading them somewhere along the Blue Ridge Parkway. We'd planned to hold a memorial service the spring after her death in Asheville, North Carolina, the city she had fallen in love with in college, for all the friends who couldn't join us in D.C. The service hasn't happened yet. First, I wasn't ready; now Virginia isn't. I don't have it in me to push the issue. Instead, I return to my books.

In *The Greek Way of Death* by Robert Garland, the author writes that the ancient Greeks practiced the thirtieth day rites, or *triakostia*, that "concluded mourning." I was afraid scattering Emily's ashes might usher in a new way of thinking about my life without her. I have not wanted the lever to switch, and my half-life to start with my forgetting. Now, I'm not sure it's even my call to make anymore. Perhaps the decision of where and when to spread Emily's ashes has passed to my children.

In the same chapter that Garland examines *triakostia*, he writes of the "kathedra," a meal "which marked the conclusion of mourning and the resumption of normal life in the community." It's easy to see the wisdom of these outward shows of one's progression through grief. And yet, at the same time, we seek pattern in the chaos, read meaning into the accidental, convincing ourselves that our dead must want to reach us. There are the odd rhyming resonances to which the bereft seem peculiarly attuned. The frequent déjà vu, the visitations, the sudden chills or heat, the whispered words in the mouths of strangers, the scents. Not a day passes in which I do not mention Emily to

Virginia and Langston, and so perhaps when they're ready, I'll take my seat at the table, but I doubt it.

One night not long after our move to North Carolina, Virginia was graced with an actual visit from Emily. In the dream, her mother came to her as she lay in bed trying not to fall asleep.

"Mommy, are you going to die?" Virginia asked her.

"Yes," Emily answered. "Would you like to see how I do it?" Then she smiled and her long arms began to give off brilliant orange sparks. Soon her whole body shimmered and disappeared into ember and fog. Virginia woke at once and joined me in my bed.

"I saw Mommy," she told me, but before I could respond, fell back asleep. In the year of Emily's death, Virginia, Langston, and I often ended up in my bed at night. A wedding gift from Emily's grandmother, the old bed had been crafted to fit the smaller people of its time. It wasn't meant to accommodate three, especially two children who preferred to sleep horizontally rather than vertically. This time, though, morning had broken long before any of us woke.

Why I've Been Out of Touch

A TIMELINE OF MESSAGES

July 10, 2007

Re: Why I've been out of touch

Hi John,

These have been the most surreal two weeks of my life. And the scariest, by far. Emily came down with an extremely rare complication called Acute Fatty Liver and came within hours of slipping into an irreversible coma. The only "cure" for this condition is to induce delivery, so Langston Nathaniel Arndt Smith, my son, was born Thursday, June 28th at 7:06 p.m. He's doing pretty well now, still in the NICU (no word on when he can come home, so we're not going to ask anymore, just take it day by day), but it was a hell of a couple of weeks. He's a good size, but is still more than a month early.

Emily is slowly getting better too, which is what they expect, but it could take a while. She got out of the hospital July 1st, but has to go back as an outpatient. Of course, we're always there anyway, staying with Langston. Her liver still measures down to her belly button and now protrudes out of the skin, but she looks a hell of a lot better than she did. It's a scary condition, though, for both her and Langston. Virginia has been a real trooper, of course.

July 14

Re: YOU

Hi Marcela,

Thank you so much for the kind thoughts. I got your phone message, but, honestly, haven't had a moment to myself. Langston is still in the NICU at Georgetown, but doing well and I think he'll be coming home the first of next week. We'll see. Emily isn't faring quite as well. She developed something called "Acute Fatty Liver syndrome." It's very rare and pretty scary, but most women are supposed to recover after delivery. Unfortunately, Emily's condition has worsened since Langston's birth and she's due to have a biopsy next week. I guess we won't know much until then.

Thank you, Marcela, for the offer of the gift of food. But, to be honest, at the moment there isn't an inch of space in the fridge or pantry. As you might imagine, once the grandparents got involved, our kitchen stopped being ours.

Here's to better days.

July 15

Re:

Hi John,

Langston is home today, free and clear of all the hospital accouterments. Emily, however, has to go in for a biopsy. Early delivery was supposed to reverse her condition, but some of the enzyme levels they measure are actually increasing, which is baffling the doctors. (Is it our destiny to be the plot of one of those doctor shows on TV.?) She feels tired and aches, but seems otherwise o.k. So far, the original diagnosis of Acute Fatty Liver stands, but who knows. It's supposed to begin to disappear after 48 hours, not become more apparent after two weeks.

We're on our third opinion now. The liver is a strong organ, though, so no one's bringing up drastic measures (unless you count the biopsy.)

It's great to have Langston home. He looks a lot like Virginia, especially in some of her more gender-neutral newborn outfits.

July 24

Re: State of things?

John,

Please keep sending kind thoughts our way. We found out yesterday that Emily has breast cancer that has spread throughout her liver. There was no problem with Langston or the pregnancy at all. We've yet to meet with the oncologist but will next week to discuss treatment. Can't quite believe I wrote that second sentence.

August 3

Re: a huge request

Dave,

I don't know how to thank you. And I'll insist on paying your gas. What we've done in the past is meet my dad at the rest stop at mile 36, south of Richmond down I-95. You'll all have cell phones, though, so meeting up shouldn't be too much of a problem. Virginia can leave at your convenience on Sunday. Thank you for this, Dave, and for all your kind thoughts and prayers. Please keep them coming.

August 3

Re: fall semester

Mr. McAleveay,

I'm afraid I won't be able to teach the two classes at George Washington I agreed to this semester. Emily was diagnosed last week with Stage IV breast cancer which has spread throughout her liver. There was never any problem with the pregnancy at all; it was always this. Her only option is chemo, which she started last week. I'm very sorry, but I simply can't be away from her this fall.

August 8

Re:

Marsaura,

The kind of cancer she has is very aggressive and hard to combat. Emily began chemo last week, and she'll be on it indefinitely. Neither surgery or radiation or other therapies are viable options at this time. We're going to Johns Hopkins for a second opinion as soon as possible. The main problem is that her liver has been partially replaced by the cancer (They weren't looking for cancer with her biopsy, but it's so widespread they found it anyway.) The tumor in her breast is small; neither she nor the doctors can feel it on examination. It's possible the pregnancy let it spread so quickly and easily, then masked the symptoms for months. She's at home now, but has a standing order to admit at Georgetown University Hospital. I'm sure she would love to talk.

August 14

Re: I haven't lost my southern manners; of course I'm gonna reply

Hey Valerie,

Thank you so much for all the lively kind thoughts and the prayers you're sending our way. We can feel 'em. I liked the article very much and will have Emily read it or, more likely, read it to her, since the Oxycodone makes her transpose her letters. Finally, she needs ME to correct HER spelling for once.

I know everyone up there is worried sick. Actually, we just got discharged from the hospital tonight, after five miserable days away from Langston and Virginia. It seems sometime last week that Emily contracted a very dangerous infection in her blood, completely unrelated to the cancer since she is not neutrapenic, but undoubtedly through an infected needle during one of her many, many biopsies and procedures. Actually, her cancer diagnosis helped us, since we were already on the lookout for fever. A healthy person might have taken some Tylenol and woke up dead (re: Jimmy Smits' character on NYPD Blue). Our hope is undiminished, but we would like to respectfully submit that two altogether separate life-threatening illnesses in as many weeks might be pushing it. At least that danger is passed, we think; all I have to do is administer the antibiotic through the medi-port in her chest for twelve days and her chemo will resume in less than a week. The real problem, of course, is that kind of cancer she has is about the worst there is, 8 of 9 on their scale. It is very aggressive and it has been feasting on her liver for months, since throughout the pregnancy, she was misdiagnosed. No blame; cancer was the furthest thing from our minds too. (Though perhaps it shouldn't have been; story upon story of women in their mid-thirties getting pregnant and getting cancer seem to be popping up, and Emily dreamed repeatedly that she had cancer in the last month of pregnancy.) It seems chemotherapy is our only option right now. Chemo and the things we're doing ourselves, which, I've come to believe, are no less significant. Can you see me as a vegetarian? I never knew there were FOUR food groups. We're also thinking about some other radical life changes, and, perhaps most significant, I'm converting to Catholicism. How's that for a radical life change? When do I learn the handshake?

Please feel free to share the salient details with anyone who's interested. Emily is amazingly strong, in body and mind and spirit, and does so much better when she's home holding Langston and scolding Virginia and indulging me. The first chemo apparently had an impact. Her liver functions showed improvement on the last tests. Once we get her liver back to normal (a tall challenge since the doc says her liver has been partially replaced by the cancer, thus surgery is off the table) she'll be eligible for some clinical trials.

Love,

Michael (Emily never liked "Mike." She should really tell me these things.)

August 17

Re: update

Hi John,

I meant to write sooner. On our discharge Wednesday, we received some encouraging news: Though her side effects have been mild, the chemo is apparently having an effect; her liver function has improved. Still a long way to go before other treatments are even to be talked about, but even the oncologist was a bit taken aback that it happened so soon. She didn't expect any measurable progress until after 2-3 treatments. And the fact that Emily's body tolerated the side effects so well generally means she will tolerate these drugs in the same way for the duration. After all, she's tolerated my side effects with aplomb for more than ten years now. Her danger seems to be anemia, not infection, which is much more manageable.

Speaking of encouraging...I want you to know how much the generosity and kindness of our dear friends in South Bend has meant. I will write to each by mail in time, but please, John, know and spread the word that we are very grateful and will never forget it. It was nice to spend a night crying tears motivated by thankfulness and joy, rather than the usual motivations.

Side notes: I've turned to reading Shakespeare of all things this past month. A little clunky to lug around, but worth it.

August 24

Re: checking in

Hey Ali,

I saw you strolling down Wisconsin with Karen the other day, but was rushed. What can I tell you? Emily has had now two rounds of chemo and has encouraged her doctor with her response. Her side effects seem so far to be limited to anemia and fatigue, which is much better than nausea and a compromised immune system. In the meantime, though, she developed a life-threatening blood infection (Her white blood cell counts have stayed normal; this could have happened to anyone.) from one of her many procedures and now I've been giving antibiotics every day through the medi-port near her heart. Scary.

You might catch me and Langston out and about now; we broke in his Bjorn carrier. Don't laugh.

August 24

Re: hey

Hey Deno,

Thank you. You know, lately I've been trying to help Emily learn the art of visualization. "If you see yourself making a three-pointer, you'll make the three-pointer." I don't think she's buying it yet; she's seen me shoot.

August 26

Re:

Thank you, Steve. I'm learning to be both forthright in my needs and dependent on the kindness of others this summer. We might, in fact, be leaving Washington, since the reason we're here, my wife's position at Georgetown, is now in jeopardy. We're hopeful, but it remains to be seen when and if she can, or will want, to return to Georgetown. In short, everything is in flux. What is constant is my willingness and desire to do anything that might relieve Emily of stress, as she begins this process of recovery.

August 28

Re: Regarding this morning

Oh goodness, Roberta, I thought no such thing. You and Chuck have been so kind and generous, I have nothing but good thoughts and a grateful heart for you both. You certainly did not appear insensitive! You're right about feeling conflicted, though Emily (heroically) and I (following as best I can her lead) are choosing now to just celebrate the joy. Latest of which: Langston has gained three and a half pounds since last month and is squarely within the normal range of full-term babies at two months. In short, he's absolutely thriving in every way.

August 30

Re: Tony again

Hey Tony,

Sorry it's taken me so long to get back to you. And thank you for your sweet thoughts. We're okay. Langston is thriving, 11 lbs at his 2 month appointment. Emily's case is a hard one. Despite this, we have hope. We've changed our diet and outlook on things and she's now had two cycles of chemo. Cancer is the only disease, apparently, for which there is no point of no return. (Enlightened oncologists don't even give timelines anymore.) Because, she's young, too young for routine mammograms actually, and strong, and Langston and Virginia give her great reason to fight, statistics don't really apply. And she surprised her oncologist with the rapidity of her response to the first cycle. I've dropped two of my courses this semester and have a new mission in life, but one of the consequences of getting out of writing for a while is that I haven't been able to follow, even from a distance, your meteoric career as much as I have wanted. I'm proud to know you, Tony, and more proud to count you as a friend.

September 2

Re: hi

Hey Carla,

Thank you, and I'm glad you got back okay. No canceled flights?

I just put Virginia down with Langston wide awake in his chair beside the bed. It worked surprisingly well. Also, I experimented with giving 6 ounces every four hours, rather than four every three or so. It's worked better, I think. We'll see if it was just the novelty of it. Em, Virginia, and I gave him a bath tonight, too.

Em seems a little better today. Eating and drinking more, if not up and about more. I don't know if depression is sapping her appetite. I do know last night was one of the low points for me. Today is better. And I'm certain that I would not have the energy or will to face this week without all your help last week. I'm in your debt forever. I'm not sure her psychiatrist will make a house call, but will check. Right now, she has an appointment for Wednesday, I think.

Thank you, again, Carla. For everything.

September 4

Re: checking in

Thank you, David.

Things are ok. A mixed bag. The chemo seems to be working a little faster than her oncologist expected, but treatment keeps getting delayed for various reasons. The latest of which, an infection of some kind, has landed Emily back in the hospital for a couple of days. This is her second bout with infection even though her white blood cell count has stayed within normal limits. They now suspect that the med-a-port they placed in her chest for the chemo may be the cause. If so, they'll have to replace it, which would mean more delays. On the plus side, the effect of the chemo so far seems, in a consulting oncologist's words, "dramatic," which they say increases the possibility of eventual remission. The problem, of course, is that it went so long undiagnosed.

September 17

Re: update

Hi John,

It's been awhile, so I thought I'd write. I wish I had encouraging news. A week ago Sunday, Emily's kidneys failed as a result of an antibiotic they gave her to combat a second blood infection. This kind of kidney failure is, apparently, reversible, but it takes a while, which means a further delay of her chemo treatment. All very frustrating. She's been in the hospital for thirteen days now, and we're all getting a little frayed. Except Langston. He continues to set records for weight gain and growth. Oh, and I now weigh what I did in high school.

September 24

Re:

Hey Mars,

Can't call now, but will keep you updated. They've started chemo again in pill form and we're hoping praying believing commanding it to have the same effect on her lungs as her liver and breast. It's a different drug (to spare the kidneys and liver) so we'll see. I've amped up the nutrition, complete with whey protein powder in the smoothies now twice a day. I thought you'd be pleased. Keep her close and dear in your thoughts.

October 16

Re:

Hey Marsaura,

Yes, Em's home. She came home last Friday. She's very weak, and there's about two hours worth of medical procedures I have to perform every day (including draining her lungs and hanging an IV bag), but she's home, and eating better, smiling more, and getting stronger every day. She hasn't started back on chemo yet because of both her physical state and because she has to finish out her course of antibiotic before resuming. The tumor in her breast has shrunk considerably and is, apparently, staying small. The bad news is that the cancer in her liver has progressed, which makes recovery slower. Dr. Liu suspects this progression is due to the delay in treatment, not that the treatment was ineffective, so we're hoping to make up ground in a couple of weeks. Life is hard, though. I have about fifteen minutes a day free from my three charges. Nancy (Did you meet her at Virginia's christening?) is in town for a week and helping with Langston, so I don't mean to bellyache, but damn…

November 5

Re: checking in

Hey Nancy,

Well, after you left, Emily continued to get stronger and stronger until the weekend before we were to meet with Dr. Liu (weekend before last), when she very suddenly started getting confused and to have pronounced tremors. Very, very scary. No fever, though, so Dr. Liu said we could wait until our appointment. At our appointment, Dr. Liu thought Em might be having another infection, so poor Em spent the rest of the week in the hospital. Turns out, she was just dehydrated, so we started chemo Saturday night in the hospital and she came home Sunday. Now, we're trying to find our routine again (and guarding against dehydration). To complicate things, I have a fairly severe case of bronchitis and Mom got sick too. We're all on the mend now, though, so keep your fingers crossed that the chemo has the effect we want and need it to have.

November 16

Re: Catching up

Hi John,

We're not sure about Emily's benefits long-term (So hard to even think long-term, but it must be done.) So far,

Georgetown has been wonderful. The benefits people have even offered to make a housecall to discuss our options, so perhaps I'll have a better handle on things next week. I'm not even sure it will come to all that; Emily is actually due a semester junior leave and it wouldn't be all that atypical to take it the 2nd semester of one's 2nd year (She has to use it sometime in her first three years), so perhaps a chat with her chair and dean would be worthwhile too. It's a hard call, and despite the fact that she's so ill and that she can't even get out of bed these days. Call me crazy, but I still have hopes that she can resume in some part her normal life. My gut tells me that all she needs is a little more time, so we're really hesitant to take a step that may prove irrevocable. The vast majority of her symptoms now are the result of the various complications and the fact that she's been bedridden for four and a half months.

Regardless of how Georgetown plays out, I will need a more substantive job, probably by spring, and I don't think I have much shot at an academic position. The likeliest thing would perhaps be some kind of entry administrative position at a college around here. Or perhaps with the NEA. George Mason is hiring a coordinator for their Fall Festival and yearly reading series. It's a full-time, year round position for which I'm well qualified, but it doesn't start until next fall and the review process begins in two weeks. Not sure I could get my act together in time. Plus, they must have innumerable graduates in the area who'd love to get the gig. I'm very open to suggestions. Again, leaving town can't be an option.

November 16

Re: Hello

Hey J,

I know this is last minute, but would you be free to grab a beer tonight, say in the next hour or so? I got the night off and am feeling like celebrating a bit (Looks like Em will be discharged tomorrow.) We could talk about

Davidson and Iona and watch some pro ball.

I would call, but my phone lost your number.

November 22

Re: Happy Thanksgiving from Georgetown...

Hey Liz,

Thank you so much for checking in; I've been meaning to touch base and say hi. I wish I had good news. Emily fell very suddenly into an hepatic coma Wednesday at 3 a.m. and is now in the ICU. She finished her chemo cycle last Saturday and was seemingly getting stronger and more and more herself. The doctors are hopeful she can turn things around and it doesn't look like the cancer is at fault here, more likely another infection.

All this to say that if you guys are free and around this Sunday sometime, I think Ginia and Langston could use a visit. If not, don't sweat it, next week would be great as well.

December 2

Re: spring

Dear _____:

I won't be teaching that class after all this spring. You'll have to contact the lit department.

December 5

Re: Bald Head

Hey Lahra,

Fran and Murray just said for you guys to pick your week and as long as it's not already rented, it's yours. My plan is to do as little as possible for a year or so, so we ought to be able to get down there to see you any week you choose.

I know Emily would want you guys to get to know the place. In fact, she'd talked about having you down next summer anyway.

December 10

Re: A hug from here to Christmas

Thank you, Valerie.

I suppose I'll tell you about it all someday. I really thought we had a chance. Numbness has set in. I seem to checking off every symptom of grieving in the little guide the hospital gives you. A textbook case. There's lots to do, and I fear I'm merely putting off a disintegration by being so busy. My one commitment is to not let my own sadness overshadow Ginia's grief. Langston will just feel a void, but Ginia...I've got to insure she doesn't associate, at least angrily and despairingly, Christmas and Thanksgiving with...Emily wouldn't want that. Myself, I hate Thanksgiving: It's when I proposed, when we lost the baby, when we checked into the hospital for the last time...

We're moving, for a while, to Cary, NC, where my folks are, then who knows...I might apply to the Kenan Emerging Writers position at Chapel Hill for next year, since it's so close. I might go on the market. I might just move to Asheville. Emily loved that town. One of only two towns she really loved for itself, DC being the other one. She always found NY a bit lonely. Plus, my two brothers and sister-in-law and niece are there. I guess I'd teach high school. Or back to DC to teach high school. I remain committed to raising the children with as little structured outside care as possible, which means some kind of school schedule for work. And

I have to work. To some degree, I realized I've been alone for the better part of a year now, and I only want to be alone. I'm very tired. I love you, and remember that weekend fondly. I fear we were trying guests.

December 30

Re: Happy New Year

Hey Lahra,

I'm sorry I'm so late in responding, but we don't have internet out at the island (usually that's a good thing) and Pop still persists in dial-up. We're heading back to Cary today, though. Christmas was tough, but we survived. It's also tough to make a decision about where to live. It'll still be Cary/Raleigh, but Asheville is very tempting. If I could just be reassured about work there.

Ginia's acting out a bit, but it's hard to tell from what exactly. No doubt everything. It'll be good for her to feel settled with all her things, I think, which is another reason to make a decision about living arrangements. Mom's place really is too small to stay there long.

January 1

Re: visit

Hi Marcela,

I'm so sorry it's taken me so long to get back to you. I'm glad the tent was a hit. Ginia loved it for about two weeks, then it went into a closet for two years. Life is hard. I should have an apartment by Feb, though, with Ginia enrolled in school and Mom nearby to help with Langston. Six months of that and then, who knows...

SHADOW TEXTS

HERE IS ONE ODD THING I have done. Since her death, I have kept my late wife's Yahoo account open. This was Emily's personal email account, the one she tried not to check when at work, though if you were a particularly promising student, she might give you the address after graduation. As far back as grad school, I would mock the adamant way she kept her work and personal lives separate. In truth, she had an ability to compartmentalize, to prioritize, that I both lacked and envied. Now, about once a month, I log in to this account and clean up the inbox, sending the automatic updates from Target, Babies-R-Us, and Patagonia to the trash.

In the beginning, I thought I might come across a friend from her childhood or adolescence who had not heard about her illness and death, but the news must have reached everyone because the only new emails sent to her account after her death were from me. Even after I met and married Jennifer, I sent Emily messages, marking Langston's and Virginia's milestones or acknowledging dates that had been important to us: wedding anniversaries, the birthdays of family members, and Emily's birthday too—what Virginia and Langston and I had done to remember the day. I sent messages on the anniversary of our first date—an occasion that took place before we admitted to ourselves that we were dating, one spring Sunday after our morning shift at the book store, when we impetuously decided to roam our deserted downtown and ended up on the steps that led up to UNC-Greensboro's old music building on Tate Street, eating Subway sandwiches.

As time passed, it seemed my stewardship of this account was another way to preserve something of Emily's voice for our children, there in the emails to classmates from high school, college, and graduate school. That preservation has been good for me as well. Reading through the saved messages has made me realize how much of her voice I miss.

As her health worsened over those four and a half months between diagnosis and death, Emily moved increasingly towards silence. At the time, I thought that might be a consequence of having to adapt to our new, unfamiliar roles as patient and caregiver, which was, if anything, a reversal of our ten years together—when every change of season seemed to wreck me for a week. Whatever she thought about her illness, she kept to herself: its roller-coaster progression and all that seemed to leer inexorably at us no matter what treatment we might try, what fresh attitude we adopted. Perhaps our new roles and the relentless pace of those months forced us into a new kind of intimacy, an intimacy that seemed to move beyond the need for speech. Her strange new inwardness didn't trouble me at first, but I confess it did eventually, and it haunted me in the year after her death. It haunts me still.

After all, our relationship had little shared silence. Sometimes, it seemed, we fell in love across a counter top, hanging on each other's words, discussing everything. We didn't know it at the time, but in those days at the bookstore, business was in a steady decline, so we had significant amounts of empty time. It seemed we would never run out of things to say. She'd moved back home to apply to grad school. I was finishing up my last year of college. We were in exuberant transition and could almost see our futures opening up before us, and we were wistful because this meant we saw, also, our inevitable separation as our initial graduate programs were states apart.

After marriage, late night talks replaced our Sunday mornings and we tried to meld our studies whenever we could. Emily's theology program introduced her to Biblical studies, so she decided to study Hebrew in addition to modern German. I was taking a course in the translation of poetry, so we began translating psalms from the Dead Sea Scrolls and then set to work on Goethe's *Faust*. After Virginia was born, we struggled to give up the late night kitchen table chats.

We'd exhaust ourselves swearing we wouldn't say another word as we lay beside each other in absolute darkness, anticipating any moment a stirring in the crib beside the bed. So when she became ill, I grew perplexed by the silence, then hurt, even though I told myself how terribly unfair I was being.

I kept things from her those months. Even before the diagnosis, I didn't tell her that about the shadow thoughts I had in my quiet hours of all that might go wrong with her and the pregnancy. When Dr. Laurin told us that, though cancer was present in her liver, Emily wasn't suffering from liver cancer, I'm embarrassed to say the first emotion I felt was relief. My smile confused Dr, Laurin, but for weeks I had been terrifying myself by secretly researching Emily's symptoms on the internet, concurring with every mistaken diagnosis she'd been given: gall bladder, spleen, fatty liver. Early that summer, just before our OB-GYN called to tell us Emily's liver enzymes were extraordinarily high and that we should go immediately to the hospital, I'd encountered liver cancer as a possible cause of Emily's symptoms. I thought Dr. Laurin was now giving us promising news.

After she began treatment, I didn't share the stories I read on the message boards I couldn't stop myself from visiting, forums dedicated to Stage IV Breast Cancer patients. In the hospital, when she asked what had happened to the patient in a neighboring room, I didn't always answer, and eventually she stopped asking.

I didn't tell her of how hard I tried to purge from my memory the scene I witnessed one evening during her longest hospital stay. In the room across the hall a middle-aged Indian woman in traditional dress (petticoat and sari) sat for hours in a hospital chair staring straight ahead. A boy and girl, both of whom looked to be under ten, sat on her lap, unmoving and solemn-eyed. No one spoke. When I went to get my evening coffee, I saw the man I presumed to be father and husband in agony on the rumpled sheets and white blanket. An oxygen mask covered his nose and mouth, but the room had been emptied of all other equipment. He was conscious, his eyes fixed on the open door, though no nurse had entered or exited the room for quite some time. He was hours, perhaps minutes, from death.

I recoiled from the scene, yet remained transfixed. Part of me resisted it as premonition; part of me took it as divine intervention: tread carefully or this will come to pass for Emily as well. That it did come to pass, that the scene around my wife's deathbed seemed similarly ritualistic and symbolic to those who witnessed it, so much so that two members of my family expressed a desire to paint us as I lay like a sickle around Emily's body on the bed, still makes me wonder what omen I failed to heed.

About once a month I find myself rereading the messages Emily sent during our time in D.C. In October of 2006, she emailed a new acquaintance to say that she had volunteered to go to the pumpkin patch with Virginia's 4K class and wouldn't be able to get "more than a utilitarian coffee" that day. A few days later, she was forced to reschedule because I was out of town for a reading, and she had to wait for a heating service to check the unit in our apartment.

That same month, two students who'd been particularly attached to her at Converse College, wrote long emails, catching her up on all the events of their lives since the previous May. One was looking at law schools in the northeast and the other had moved to New York to work for a publishing house. Both made it clear that their lives wouldn't have taken them in these directions had they not encountered her. Their exuberance, their desire to impress her and to let her know just how much she had meant to them seemed to embolden the fonts as I read. "It's completely fascinating, and it's exactly something I can picture learning about in one of your classes," one writes. "You were so right to encourage me to bigger and better things than Spartanburg. I'm so unbelievably happy here, both in New York and at this place in my life. I sort of feel like the entire world is at my fingertips, MUCH closer than it would have been from a desk in admissions at Converse."

Emily's response was her all over. "I love to hear about it all," she writes after lamenting she can't be more "newsy" because she's completely swamped. She wants them to know, though, that she is "...well, proud is not the word, as it is your effort and not mine, but I am happy about your choices and your future." Then, she finds the time to make the message newsier than she expected. "I think of you often, too...am planning a class and writing project about women, religion, and memoir in a year or two, and I will always associate you with that work because of our time at Converse."

What must have gone through Emily's mind was just how similarly she and I had been feeling since moving to D.C. three months before. Substitute D.C. for New York, and the email from her student might have been one that Emily herself composed to *her* mentor. After all, only nine months had passed since we'd made the trip back to South Bend so that Emily could defend her dissertation. We, too, had arrived that summer in a big city, having started jobs that seemed perfectly structured to support us in any project that captured us. Excess—we were feeling it in a way we'd never felt before.

Many of the emails from that first semester, though, revolve around Virginia and me, small family discoveries, explorations of our new city, the nights out at Kavanagh's pizza and at Max's Ice Cream, where Virginia bravely tried a scoop of pumpkin-spice for the first time and fell in love with the taste. There's a huge gap in the emails from December to April. Though difficult months for Emily, both physically and mentally, they were also full. She'd been put on bed rest in March because of her digestive problems and history of late miscarriages, and preferred to communicate with students and colleagues by phone.

Easter Sunday, Emily broke her silence to write a long message to her friend, Janice, a fellow theologian from graduate school. Janice's husband and Emily had constituted their year's class in ethics, and the four of us had grown close. Later, when Emily was pregnant with Virginia, Janice became her go-to person for help in navigating the demands of pregnancy and childbirth with the strain of teaching for the first time. It was Janice who recommended we take classes teaching the Bradley method of natural childbirth, which had helped make Virginia's birth so magically difficult. Of her pregnancy with her unnamed son, Emily wrote that Easter Sunday:

> Busy is the nature of these days of our lives, isn't it? I
> hope yours has been a mostly happy busy—that the

boys, and you and Bill are all healthy and doing well. Catch me up when you have some "spare" time. We are doing pretty good here...very busy and all that. Our biggest news is that I am pregnant again...our BOY is due the first of August. So far, so good. Some pains and other small problems so I am staying off my feet as much as possible (as you must know this is easier said than done). And some very small worries from the ultrasound but we are trying to trust all will be resolved and turn out wonderfully. He is very active and responsive to everything already.

It's particularly hard to read and reread this one, in light of what happened and I can't help but compose shadow texts as palimpsest beneath Emily's words. By this time, she'd been on bed rest for almost a month and her phrase "the pains and other small problems" was too brave a way of referencing the agony and deep worry. Two and a half months later, as she and I traveled by ambulance from Sibley Hospital, where she'd been slated to give birth, to Georgetown because the facility was more equipped to handle the emergency induction, I wondered how she could go through a natural delivery when she was so clearly exhausted.

Five years before, we'd written an intricate birth plan, specifying for example, that Bach's Cello Suites play during the first stage. But we had not foreseen the forty-plus hours of labor Emily would endure before Virginia arrived. With Langston's birth, we learned the urgency of the situation only after arriving at Georgetown, and it would be another thirty-six hours until labor, time Emily spent suffering the low-grade discomforts of assessment and monitoring. I remember thinking, as we arranged care for Virginia and rushed to Sibley, that I would have to make it up to Emily after Langston arrived. She'd suffered so much for our family, and my temper had been growing shorter and shorter with her. Even today, I flush with shame when I remember joking to a friend (Can I really have said this?) that I wanted my next partner to be a more practiced stoic.

In an email dated April 10th, Emily wrote to my sister-in-law about her newfound commitment to live in the present. And I remember discussing this with her one night around the same time.

Virginia had finally fallen to sleep and we'd opened the window in the kitchen. Emily and I were sitting at our dining room table, luxuriating in the cool spring air and watching our dog, Jane, scamper and spin in response to the evening noises outside. Earlier that evening, I'd seen a mother raccoon, who'd made her home in one of the courtyard's tall oaks, scamper to the gutter, and mentioning it to Emily, quoted a line from a poem I'd written that she'd helped me with. "...Animal drift of the eternal present." This self-quoting was a mildly annoying habit of mine that I've since broken, though at the time, Emily stopped me gently with one of her sly smiles. This is the last night we were something like our old selves together. Soon after, she wrote:

I am a little starved, stuck in my apt. with only Michael and Virginia (and then Anne) to talk to. Think I am a little crazy (and I think a little angry and not very honest with myself about that). Anyway, maybe we (read: I) will be able to talk about other things next time...I can't wait until next summer when we will be able to visit you guys up there. I can't believe I haven't seen your pretty place yet!

My new strategy (I'll let you know how it works out) is to try to see things more long-term. Not looking to the future for happiness (I am trying to live in the moment MORE) but to realize there will be plenty of time for lots of good things...that this period (mommy days) will last awhile and there will be other summers...

The subsequent message to my sister-in-law on April 19th breaks me in two.

I found myself with a few minutes before it is time for a pregnancy check-up this morning, so thought I'd email. Present to the moment...a wonderful goal, but pretty hard I think. I am not good at it at all. My new attempt to see the big picture or whatever is working ok, especially with work. But I have not been "present" to my own moments and certainly not to Michael...but we are working on it.

This message breaks me not because I'm foolish enough to think that, had I to go through it all again, I could somehow preserve our old ways of being together, but because I realize how much I stayed in my Emily's thoughts, even when her discomfort and worry leap off the page at me now.

One week from our anniversary, and exactly two weeks before Langston will be induced, Emily writes to another old friend, one who will become indispensable to me over the next few years as I wrestle with the bureaucracy that accompanies widowers and single parents:

> Things are ok here.... I developed gall bladder trouble in the last week or so and lost a lot of time and energy to feeling really rotten and going to the Doc. I think it is slowly getting better (though I have had to cut out all fat from my diet, which is much harder than I expected... not craving, but just thinking of things I can eat beyond fruit and veggies). But baby seems to be fine...at least that worry is getting better all the time.
>
> Today is Virginia's last day of school, so I guess this afternoon she is a kindergartener! Crazy. Anne and Frank are coming early next week for a visit. I really hope it goes well...hope I feel like enjoying the company and hope Anne and I get along well...I've become very sensitive (easily irritated?) by things so have to hope hard.

The next email shocked me when I first read it because I hadn't noticed the date it was sent—August 4, twelve days after her Stage IV breast cancer diagnosis. She's writing to the same friend to confirm her plans to visit and help:

> This will be quick as am dopey and achy but all generally ok today. All your thoughts and notes mean so much.
>
> The dates you suggested look great at this point—especially the 26th of August through the first of September or so—things of course change...I hope to go to Johns Hopkins for a second consultation, as yet unscheduled. Aug 27 V's first day and the 30th is another chemo session.
>
> I hope a little of this makes sense b/c I can't sit here anymore.

The voice of the last email sent from the account takes me out of the place I go every time I dip back into these messages. The voice, its mechanical hope, repels me because it is not Emily's, but my own. As always, I was in a rush and so used Emily's account to more quickly find the address of another old friend who was coming into town to help.

> It's too late to call, so this will have to do. Emily was admitted back into the hospital today for a possible infection and they're likely to keep her there for at least a couple of days. We'll know more tomorrow. I know it's hard not to have your stomach sink when you hear about these things, but the doctors seem to take this in stride and keep telling us that we're just going to have to find a way to get through these niggling hiccups, always keeping the bigger picture in mind.
>
> And there have been encouraging developments. The chemo is working. One of her enzymes is now within normal limits and they're pretty sure the effect on the cancer has been "dramatic." For my part, I can tell you her liver, which once extended below her navel, is now back up where it's supposed to be under her ribcage. The ER docs thought so too.
>
> All this means that you might be on your own getting from the airport to our apartment....Someone will be there to let you in, but it probably won't be me....Call our number when you get there, and someone will either come down or toss you the keys from the window.

It's increasingly hard for me to justify keeping up this account. What am I honoring by preserving my late wife's emails from our time in D.C. other than the pathos of our blindness? It feels like a spiritual act, this stewardship, but to what god am I attempting to bring pleasure? Or am I worshipping some new goddess, our goddess of hypertext, whose presence is felt by the lightning flash firing of the occipital nerve in heads bent too long over illuminated screens? If so, what prayer of mine could she answer?

Play Dates

THE FIRST TIME my daughter Virginia and I arrived at Jennifer's house, the rain had been coming down unrelentingly for hours. It was mid-January and miserably cold, and we were there for the Monday afternoon play date we would keep once a week until Jennifer and I married two and a half years later. The rain that first day was one of those downpours I associate with tropical climates, a rain that was more sound than sensation. There was no wind, and the fat, splashy drops darkened the tree trunks and greened even the shady patches on the lawn. The sloped roof of Jennifer's house had become a snare drum, her gutters a shekere, as small sheets of water flowed down the drive into the street. The world felt raw, which suited my mood.

I could tell Virginia was more nervous than excited, and I wondered if it was because I'd insisted on tagging along. At five and a half, she was entering a stage of wanting a social life of her own. She'd known the family for more than a month, and spent several easy Sunday afternoons with Jennifer's three children, William, Emily, and Katie on the church playground. She'd even met the children's father, Jennifer's ex.

Jennifer directed the children's services at the Episcopal Church my mother attended and had been very kind to Virginia since I'd sent her and my six-month-old son Langston to my parents soon after Emily's funeral mass, so that I might get my grades in for the semester and pack up our apartment. Having heard of my wife's death from a fellow parishioner, Jennifer had made sure to include Virginia at church, making sure she got dibs for snacks and toys, and had even invited her to explore with her a couple of the many city parks.

So on our first playdate at Jennifer's house, I was the newcomer, an interloper, the one most likely to disrupt whatever provisional hierarchy childhood shyness and sympathy had already constructed among the four kids. Katie, who was ten, and Emily, who was eight, were sweeter to Virginia than they might have been had her sad story not proceeded her. Katie made a point of picking Virginia as teammate first for games, which prompted in my daughter such feelings of admiration that they would persist through even the turmoil of a new marriage and move. William, who was younger than Virginia by a mere month, was simply happy to have someone his age to play with.

The first memory I have of this first playdate is seeing through the front doorway Emily and William sitting together on the white carpet of the small living room, just after Jennifer answered the door. The two children were playing Dig Dug on a joystick that plugged directly into the television, a video game from my own childhood. William began his turn, digging through the levels of orange dirt.

He turned briefly when he heard us enter and chirped "Hi" in his clipped, squirrel-like way. Looking back on this scene, the conventional pleasures it suggests unnerve me. It still felt wrong to be apart from Langston even for an afternoon, and the ordinary challenges of my new life as single parent loomed larger by the day. Virginia's mother had been dead for a little over a month.

"Emily. Say 'hello'," Jennifer reminded her daughter.

What happened next would continue without warning for months, for years. I knew Jennifer's second daughter's name was Emily, but hearing it spoken aloud did something to me. Whatever civility required of me in the next few minutes—a smile, handshake, or high five—was beyond me. At hearing the name Emily, my mind sputtered and I couldn't for a moment put it right again. I needed a place to crash down and recover, and so I moved directly to the couch, feigning imperative interest in the game.

"I haven't seen this game in a long time. Watch out! Here comes the fire."

On the screen, a green Frygar engulfed Dig Dug in a blossoming jet of flame.

"My turn," Emily yelled. William handed over the joystick and ran to his room for Legos.

I felt a cold sweat coming on and was grateful for the rain. I kept the conversation light and spoke of the three months that Emily and I'd spent in Roanoke after we were married. Our first day I'd found an old Elevator Action arcade game in the back room of a rundown convenience store up the road from our apartment. What luck! How could I not have taken this discovery for a sign? When I was a boy, I'd spent every Saturday morning I could at Putt-Putt Golf and Games, where for ten dollars I got eighty tokens, a slice of cheese pizza, and a drink. I fed Elevator Action most of my tokens, wasting hours trying to make it to the bottom of that elevator shaft. I spent every free afternoon that Emily was working at that store.

Virginia had been introduced to video games late in her childhood and wasn't much interested in watching the screen, just as later she would prove much less interested in the world of iPhones and apps than her friends and siblings. That first day she sat on the couch chatting with Jennifer and me. Honestly, I was relieved. Since we'd moved to North Carolina, it had been hard for me to let my daughter out of my sight. I insisted on accompanying her even to the courtyard outside our apartment, and took her out of school more often than I should have. This phenomenon perplexed me, especially since I seemed able, albeit grudgingly, to leave Langston with my parents for an afternoon or evening or during my irregular short mornings of work. He wasn't quite crawling yet, so caring for him meant learning a routine and keeping watch for only the expected. Perversely, Virginia seemed much more vulnerable.

Once spring arrived, the afternoon play dates moved outside. As a father of young children, I was surprised that I found playing with the older children so satisfying. Katie and Emily already knew the rules to any game I might propose, so I could invest more fully in playing to win without guilt. The front yard of Jennifer's house was large and flat, bound at one end by an old oak tree and a minor forest of shrubs at its base. Two crepe myrtles stood sentry on either side of the front walk, and an overgrown forsythia that would bloom so spectacularly that summer infiltrated the backyard fence. The yard was perfect for team sports, and soccer was the game of choice, the teams breaking down, most often, along family lines—Jennifer's three children versus Virginia and myself. The only complication with this arrangement was that Virginia, playing goalie, thought she could tell when I was going easy on the kids, and like any good coach, wanted my full effort every time.

On rainy days, Jennifer was happy to spend the entire afternoon talking with me on the couch. Almost from the beginning, I felt more comfortable discussing Emily's death with her than with any of my friends and family, perhaps because they'd been there with me when it all went wrong. It took months for me to realize how much I came to count on these play dates as one of the pleasurable fixtures in the new life I was living.

By summer, I'd begun to look so forward to my time with Jennifer and the kids that I planned my regular trips to visit friends in D.C. or Emily's parents in Greensboro around these Monday afternoons. The play dates had expanded to include supper, either out at a Shy-family-favorite pizza joint across town or fast food picked up and taken on a picnic to a nearby park or back home in the backyard. On those Mondays, time seemed to suspend and I put off the drive home to our apartment, pushing back further and further our nighty routine of bath, books, and songs. Jennifer's house had become refuge, holding reality at bay.

It was late January a full year later before I finally realized what I had gradually been feeling for weeks. I don't remember experiencing any of the embarrassments of past love affairs, the sweating over minor details of schedule and appearance. Instead, I felt a ripening of feeling, though my heart was not quite awake to the fact that I was showing signs of life. Even now, I wonder whether Jennifer experienced something similar. She told me once after we were married that her friends had advised her to give up on me as a partner, that I wasn't "there" yet and might never be. Did she worry that our roles had already been established, friends to the end? I've always been somewhat clueless to romantic cues, but at some point I recognized what I was feeling.

Alone, at night, I began to give the arc of my friendship with Jennifer a Shakespearian revision. It was if we'd found ourselves suddenly free and in charge of what was left of our lives. Together, we would have to find our way, a way to care for these five children who grounded and sustained us, who always gave us another occasion to meet again or extend our time together. We'd each seen our share of suffering, but the story was being written before our eyes, plot lines entwining, a braid of sorrow and passion.

Virginia, always sensitive to the life and language of adults, noticed first.

"Are you and Jennifer going to get married?" she asked me one evening on our way home.

"No, honey. What made you ask that?"

"Why not? You already sit beside each other on the couch."

Over the months, I'd moved across the room from the chair opposite Jennifer to join her on the couch for our weekly talks. Had I been absent-mindedly flirting, leading her on? Did I mean it? More than a year after Emily's death, I still went at my days distractedly, unconscious to everything but vague feelings of guilt on Monday nights, guilt that had been giving way, gradually, to anticipation for Wednesdays, the next time I could count on seeing Jennifer at the children's choir rehearsal. The exchanges we had before and after rehearsal became continuations of whatever we'd talked about two days earlier. Having established a tradition of saving the Sunday crossword to work on together but never finish Monday afternoon, we each completed our puzzles alone on Tuesday to compare our results on Wednesday. Increasingly, my first and last thoughts of the day were of her, and we picked up now in public wherever we'd left off in what passed for the privacy of her couch, beset on all sides by little voices.

"You're right, Virginia, we do," I said. "Is that okay?"

She didn't speak, but smiled and turned to watch an airplane wink its lights out her window.

The following Monday, I resolved to tease out Jennifer's feelings. How could I trust myself when I was still trying to figure who I was and what I should be doing with what still felt like a half-life? I went to her house prepared with an elaborate story. Katie had guided Langston to the kitchen and the other three were out of sight and mind, playing wizard school in one of the back bedrooms when we sat down on the couch.

"My mom has been trying to fix me up with the daughter of a friend of hers," I said.

Jennifer's face betrayed nothing.

"We have, ostensibly, a lot in common. She's smart and pretty, loves literature, a professor. But something isn't right." Was that a flicker of relief flashing across her face as I spoke? "Maybe I'm just not ready."

After an uncharacteristically long pause, she said, "That could be, or perhaps you're closer than you think." How could this house so full of people suddenly become so quiet? It couldn't stay that way for long, of course. A sudden clatter in the kitchen drew Jennifer to her feet in a rush. Luckily, I knew enough to follow her. William and Virginia and Emily were chasing each other through the house and had bumped the plastic play kitchen where one-and-a-half-year-old Langston was knocking the pots and pans to the floor. Instinctively, Jennifer picked him up, thinking he'd been hurt.

"Come on, guys, let's go outside," I said.

The day was cool, but sunny and dry. I suggested a game of tag or hide-and-go-seek, but Virginia wanted to play "Tree." In this game, I stood like a body-builder, legs apart, arms out to my side and crooked at the elbow, while she climbed up my torso to perch on my bicep. She held onto my wrist as I bent with the breeze. This time William climbed, too, so I held them both for as long as I could.

"Now, let's do flips," Virginia said. William and Emily quickly joined in. Holding my hands, the three of them took turns walking up my body until they somersaulted and landed on their feet in the grass. I added to the thrill by raising my hands a little as they climbed, so that by the end they were airborne. Jennifer came out as we started the second rotation. She held Langston on her hip in that nonchalant way moms alone seem to have. I caught her eye and cocked an eyebrow—There was a question I needed answered, though

I hadn't asked it exactly. Almost imperceptibly, she nodded, smiling as Langston's sobbing subsided at the strange sight of Virginia walking up his daddy's chest to launch out and flip to the ground. Even eight-year-old Emily squealed when she landed.

Jennifer walked over to me to give Langston a better view, laughing as the kids lined up for another turn. The height wasn't great, but for a moment the kids were falling, in a loop caught by gravity, returned breathless and safe to their world.

There We Are

In January 2009, one year after my wife's death, I gave up the comfy apartment that had been home for the last year and moved in with my parents. They lived outside Raleigh in one of those bland and cavernous new houses identical to its neighbors. The cut-peppermint sidewalks curling around the edged and overfed lawns made it seem like we were living inside the sugar decoration of an enormous sheet cake.

It was a strange place to find myself groping toward life again, but I was. The children and I found a drainage pond hidden by hedges near the big rocks at the neighborhood's edge, and from then on, our evening walks included slipping behind the bushes to skip pebbles across the water's orange surface. A small trail passed through what remained of the cleared forest at the end of a cul-de-sac, where we might spy deer or, more likely, hear them crash through the distant underbrush. Once, early that spring, Virginia and I stumbled upon a fawn, so young it trembled, not ten feet from where we'd been skipping blithely along. It took us a moment to notice the mother beside her baby, her frozen stare. For what seemed like minutes, the four of us locked eyes with one another. Then the doe began moving gingerly away, and after a moment's hesitation, the fawn picked its way after, disappearing behind a veil of leaves. I think Virginia and I both took it as a sign that home might be anywhere we found ourselves with those we loved.

The last time I'd lived with my parents for any length of time had been my final semester of college. Emily and I were engaged the Thanksgiving before and I'd used most of my financial aid money that semester to purchase the engagement ring. I'd chafed a bit living under my parents' roof then, so this time around I was surprised at how easily and quickly we all fell into an easy routine. Mom found a preschool nearby willing to take Langston mid-year, where he could go three mornings a week, and that, along with Virginia's school schedule, gave new shape to my days.

For the first time in almost two years, I had time for writing or talk after the early morning bustle. On off days, Langston and I tried to get out of the house so my father, who worked nights, might sleep undisturbed. Because I didn't want to switch Virginia to yet another school mid-year, we commuted fifteen miles each morning to our old neighborhood where she'd started school in September, and, sometimes, Langston and I spent the day in the neighborhood, meeting Jennifer for lunch or making a tour of the library and playground. We both preferred the great, sprawling park near his preschool, though. As often as not, he took his morning nap while we made the trip back home to my parents' new house.

A good-sized lake bordered the park, and the road to Langston's school crossed it, bisecting the water into uneven halves, resembling a blown-up balloon twisted at one end. I remember the precise moment (is this a recognizable milestone in a toddler's development?) when Langston grew aware enough of his place in the world to point out one window, then the other, as we crossed the little bridge, and shout "Big water!" then squeak, "Tiny water!" We would stop at the standard playground of plastic slides and tunnels and swings to play pirates, but even at twenty months Langston preferred the trails that snaked around the lakeshore. He put up with my goofing around on the outdoor amphitheater stage and conversing with the Tolkienian Ent-face someone had carved into an oak. In return, I filled my pockets with as many sweet gum pods as possible. We headed to the bank and spent the morning tossing the pods into the water and watching them gently make their way back.

Like those gum pods in the water, I often felt more borne by life than bearing it, but the currents that moved me through my days were becoming gentler. Jennifer and I were finding our way toward a future that seemed increasingly possible and real. There was something new in the air that winter. I felt it as I stood under the streetlight at the edge of my parents' house, where I would walk to call Jennifer after the kids were asleep. I felt it sipping wine with Jennifer on the glider of her back patio. Our dates usually still began as play dates, and we saved the private things we wanted to say to one another until after bedtime. I'd spent over a year trying to be as solid and available to the other people in my life as Emily had been to the people in hers—my children, my parents, and in-laws—and that somehow kept me moving and breathing and, sometimes, let me sense something of my old self. Still, it was a shock to realize that someone who was by nature so solid and present to every moment wanted to make herself available to me.

By that summer, I could almost take for granted our shared suppers and nights, carefree routines punctuated by the occasional inter-family camping trip. Finally, the L.L. Bean tent that Emily and I had received as a wedding gift got some use. I felt so much myself again that I thought I might try the academic job market in the fall. It had been a year and a half since I'd been in the classroom. (The marathon season of hiring in higher education meant it would be another year, even if I managed to land a tenure-track job.) Still, I was writing again, and, more pertinently, money was growing short. Neither my parents nor Jennifer seemed too concerned about the possibility that I would have to leave the state for a job. The burst bubble of the housing market must have made success seem a remote possibility. The fact was that, without realizing it, I'd come to see my life in Raleigh more rooted each day.

For Virginia's seventh birthday in July I somewhat rashly bought her a rabbit. While she spent the week at Emily's parents' house in Greensboro, I had plenty of time to construct the indoor hutch. I found "Peanut" through the SPCA. He was an adult rabbit who'd been the victim of a larger rabbit's attack. The week before, he'd had two surgical shunts placed on his back to help his wounds drain, but when I picked him up the day before Virginia came home, he seemed perfectly curious and unafraid about everything, especially the fingers of an eighteen-month-old Langston, which looked temptingly like baby carrots.

It was the first time since Emily's death that Virginia had been away from us all and she'd missed home so much that, when she returned, she wouldn't leave us to go upstairs to her room. I had to pretend to be upset with her from some small trifle and told her to follow me upstairs, where she immediately discovered Peanut.

"Is it for me?" she asked me when he hopped, nose twitching, to the wire mesh at the front of the cage.

One of Virginia's most endearing characteristics is her genuine gratitude for anything she's been given. You can almost see her happiness waking within her. It breaks my heart every time I see it.

"Of course, baby!" I laughed. "Happy birthday! Would you like to hold him?"

"Can I?" She replied, then plopped down, crisscross applesauce, in front of the cage and stretched out her arms. I opened the front door that, when lowered, became a ramp. Peanut hopped down immediately and into the trampoline that the skirt of her dress formed over her crossed legs. Her entire body seemed charged with joy.

Peanut would survive the move we'd make to Mississippi and live another four years, letting himself be bathed in kisses by the dog and terrifying the two cats when we let him out for exercise and play. We buried him under the magnolia tulip tree that grows outside Virginia's bedroom, the tree, with its thick, low branches, that eight-year-old Virginia used to climb to feel close to her mother during our first few years here. The first time I spotted her in there, her face turned skyward shone with tears as she talked loudly to her mother, I watched from her window but had learned enough about the necessity of grief not to intrude.

But before Mississippi and after Jennifer and I'd been dating for almost a year it became clear that the older girls, Katie and Emily, were taking our ripening relationship hard. Increasingly that winter, they retreated to their rooms when Virginia, Langston, and I came over. Once I understood that this wasn't some new, mysterious phase of early adolescence, I asked Jennifer for permission to talk to them, so one evening after the usual routine of supper choir rehearsal, Jennifer asked me to drive the girls home, while the three younger children stayed behind to help her prep for Sunday school.

"So guys," I began slowly. "I've noticed we don't have much to do with each other anymore."

Silence.

"I miss our games. It's fun to play with the little kids but not the same. They're not as good as you guys are."

Not even the flicker of a smile. I kept trying, taking the long way to their house and even looping around the block. Finally, Katie spoke.

"Can we just go home?"

"Fine," I snapped, instantly angry at myself for showing my temper.

My relationship with Katie and Emily remained in a kind of stasis, but Jennifer and I grew closer. While on one of our family camping trips, I brought up marriage. Our five children were sleeping in their tent, and Jennifer and I were talking and drinking around the fire. She was concerned about being away from a dear friend who'd just given birth. I was concerned about my dwindling job prospects. Suddenly, as the fire eased to a steady smolder, I heard myself saying, "Perhaps we ought to get married." I felt her say "yes" before her mouth spoke the word.

Though the girls were, predictably, resistant to speaking with a counselor, we wanted them to have help coming to terms with the impending blend of our families. Jennifer and her ex had been living apart for several years, but Katie and Emily knew that the divorce between hadn't been finalized, and naturally enough, had been holding onto the hope that their parents might get back together. Second marriages are always likely to be more fraught and bittersweet than first ones, especially when children are involved, but this revelation hit me hard. Who was I to force heartbreak onto them? Shouldn't I have been the one to step back to give them the time they needed? It hadn't occurred to me that the possibility of a new beginning for me might mean the end of possibility for Jennifer's children.

Just what this new life together might look like, we didn't know. I'd applied for work up and down the East Coast and as far west as the Mississippi river, having promised my family I would look no farther than a day's drive or so from North Carolina. But I hadn't had much luck, and Jennifer and I returned from that camping trip assuming we would somehow make things work where we were. She would put her small house on the market, we would find a place to rent large enough for our blended family, and I would find at least part-time work at nearby community colleges.

In May, though, I received a call from the chair of the Division of Languages and Literature at Delta State University. Jennifer's first reaction was that I should turn down his offer of a campus visit. This first substantial disagreement showed in relief, I think, the opposing traits of our personalities: her tendency to stick to a plan even in the face of the unforeseen and my inconvenient impulsivity, which led me to instantly seize on new possibilities as perfect solutions. In the end, Jennifer agreed to go with me, and I agreed to put off any decision until we'd returned to North Carolina after.

Soon after I signed the letter accepting the position Jennifer noted, wryly, that I'd managed to keep my promise to my family: we would be living east of the Mississippi, even if only by fifteen miles. We were on the brick patio of her little Raleigh home, readying the place for the open house her realtor had arranged for the next day—and as the agent had requested, were pulling up years of weeds and mosses that had settled between the bricks—all seven of us. The work was hard and gritty, smack dab in the middle of summer. Though it was late, the bricks were still warm from the sun and the dirt packed and dry. Katie thought to use the hose and the water brightened everything it hit, the bricks, the dirt, and, inevitably, our seven glistening selves.

We were scowling and laughing, thinking about supper, and what Friday night movie to watch. At one point, I looked up and caught the sight of us in the reflection of the house's kitchen windows. In my mind, this scene has become yet another snapshot of my life, an image refracted in such unpredictable ways by the years since, as if my world really did move according to strange laws just beyond the limits of my understanding. There we are, two families broken apart, working hard at becoming something new and whole, a *mise en abyme* bound by love beneath the apparent chaos of coming together.

Tell Me What You Want and I'll Tell You Who You Are

"A Dreary Story"

—Anton Chekov

Because there is much about my stepdaughter Emily to admire, too often, I have to remind myself not to let my hope that she'll do great things with her life shade, unfairly, into conviction and belief. Once, during her months of chemo while an inpatient at St. Jude, a social worker told Jennifer that the experience, as difficult as it was, would undoubtedly change her daughter, that undergoing treatment for cancer would make her a better person, and she was right. Over the last two years, Emily has grown much more patient and compassionate, which is all the more remarkable since the passing of these two years have thrust her into the middle of her adolescence.

Emily's instinctive strong sense of justice buttresses her new compassion, which means she hasn't softened into sentimentality, I'm happy to say. She is in the throes of high school now, where admiration often masquerades as fear. Her formidable sense of right and wrong often intimidates her classmates, so it has become her fate in our small town to be well-known but not popular, which suits her. She has one loyal friend who complements her nicely, adding the yins of mellowness and good humor to Emily's yang of a cast-iron will.

Conversely, I was all but anonymous in high school and lacked distinction in just about every way. Although my first wife, Emily, walked the same halls that I did, laughing with some of the same people who were friendly to me, we somehow never crossed paths. I'm grateful that this is so. I was a mess, and so less sure of who I was than either of my stepdaughters. Once, in ninth grade, I cracked my head on my own locker during the five minutes we had between third and fourth period, knocking myself senseless. I had to be half-carried by two of my classmates to the office where the fat and balding assistant principal wouldn't stop laughing at me long enough to call my mother. This is why I say to Virginia and Langston that it was lucky their mother and I didn't meet in high school when the kids ask how it was that we could have spent three years in the same place without catching sight of one another.

The truth is I envy my stepdaughter her poise. And yet Emily was, at times, a problematic patient for a medical staff who must have been trained to deal with problem patients. Often, especially early on, she made snap judgments about a doctor or nurse and simply refused to respond to their direct questions, and then the following day seemed unaware that anyone might have found anything amiss about her behavior.

As I did, during my first wife's illness, Emily appreciated directness in her caregivers, rather than the sugary, euphemistic speech some medical professionals adopt. Greeting her with a question like "And how are we feeling this morning?" turned her off completely, and guaranteed she'd give that asker the silent treatment for the rest of the shift.

Jennifer, long used to Emily's tactics of passive resistance, was less mortified than resigned, and more willing than I would have been to let her work out on her own her relationships with the kind staff at St. Jude. It must have been difficult for some of them, enduring Emily's defiance and scorn when they'd just come from administering to a child who wouldn't live to see her adulthood, or her next birthday, or another full moon. As terrifying and traumatic as those four months were for Emily, the nurses knew that she would in all likelihood recover completely and go on to live a full, 21st century American life.

In fact, the largest worry turned out to be not the cancer, but the potential lingering and long-term effects of the chemotherapy, which might damage everything from her lungs to her hearing. Luckily, all that the chemotherapy seems to have done has been to change her black hair from wavy to downright curly. In the three years since treatment, she's grown it out, and she's lovely, so classically beautiful that I suspect she must intimidate into silence anyone her age who might like to get to know her better. And that is just as well. She shows little interest in romantic relationships—little interest, in fact, in most of the social activities of high schoolers in our small town. Like a lot of adolescents, she spends most of her free time in her room, entering the spheres of our awareness unpredictably and with the alacrity of a pistol shot, as if to say, "Wake up! This is life!" before returning as quickly to her own private world to which even our two cats, the faithful companions of most of her childhood, are less and less privy.

In the fall of 2011, after Emily returned home and life could begin again for us all in our new hometown, the Delta coordinator for Make-a-Wish foundation phoned to set up a meeting the following week. She paid a house call one weekday evening to discuss Emily's options in making her wish. The meeting was an education for the entire family. The coordinator was a agreeable, chatty woman who'd obviously been doing her job for some time. I sent the rest of the children to play in their rooms while Jennifer invited the coordinator to have a seat with Emily on the couch.

The first misconception the woman corrected for us was our idea that the Make-a-Wish foundation catered only to children with illnesses that would likely prove fatal. Indeed, the foundation aims to serve any child diagnosed with a serious, chronic illness, which, of course, qualified Emily. "Now, we need to make sure that the wish is what the child wants, not what Mom or Dad want," she continued. "You would not believe some of the things I've heard: wishes for new cars or swimming pools!"

For that reason, she explained, experiences were much more likely to be granted than wishes for tangible items. Meeting Taylor Swift, for instance, would be feasible, although something like that might take a little time to arrange.

"Especially since Emily is healthy again!" the coordinator said, cheerily. "Honey, you might have to wait awhile if the Foundation has to 'prioritize' a more serious case."

While I was registering what "prioritizing" meant in this context, she turned to Emily and asked her if she'd like Jennifer and me to leave the room. When Emily declined, the coordinator paused, as if determining whether or not to proceed, before asking Emily if she'd thought about for what she might wish. When the woman asked again, she again only received a sheepish shrug and smile. She wondered once more if, perhaps, Emily would feel more comfortable expressing her wish in private. No, Emily simply could not think of anything she might want.

In the week leading up to the visit, she'd thought about a room makeover but changed her mind. She'd thought that she might like to arrange a trip back to Raleigh to spend the weekend with some old friends in a fancy hotel, but we'd told her that we could arrange that for her. Her sister Katie wanted her to ask for a trip to California, but that didn't appeal either.

Finally, Jennifer asked if it might be possible for Emily to give her wish to another sick child. "It's possible," the coordinator said. "But I'd want Emily to think on it for a while."

Emily asked what some of the other kids in our region had wished. At this, the woman's expression saddened. "One kid around here asked for a shopping spree at the local Walmart," she said. "He couldn't imagine doing anything beyond the Delta. We tried to dress it up some. We took him in a limo and threw in a dinner, but that's what he wanted. It about broke my heart."

Though I haven't thought about it in months, I realize that, to date, the problem of Emily's wish has yet to be resolved. What child ignores such an offer? What child refuses to even refuse such an offer? Emily's instinctive resistance to satisfying the expectations of others continues to bemuse rather than discomfit me. Sometimes it seems she is a real-life Bartleby, preferring not to distinguish between desires and needs and often refusing to acknowledge either.

Is there a time limit to making a wish? An expiration date? Would it upset Emily if we found out that her wish could no longer be granted?

IN OUR TOWN

IN THE FALL OF 2013, my daughter Virginia and her stepsister Emily were cast in the university's production of *Our Town*. The choice of play dismayed the more earnest of the students active in the Theater Program who'd applauded the provocative and contemporary choices of the previous two years. Yet I saw the subtle wisdom of putting on a play sure to interest the larger community of Cleveland, Mississippi. Because *Our Town* calls for a cast of a large range of ages, younger actors and community members were encouraged to participate. If Emily and Virginia were excited to audition, they were thrilled to have been awarded parts.

Because the director, also named Michael, was a colleague, I knew before my daughters that they were going to be in the show. He dropped by my office the morning before the cast list was sent out. "So I'm thinking about casting Virginia in a couple of small roles. She doesn't have a lot of lines, but she's on stage a long time. Emily's in high school, so I'm not worried too much about her, but will Virginia be up to the late rehearsals?"

"Not sure," I said. "She's only eleven. But she'd never forgive me if I said no."

If you're born before 1960, it's likely you know something of the play, which is set between 1901 and 1913 in Grover's Corner, New Hampshire, a fictional town that supposedly lies "42° 40' north latitude and 70° 37' west longitude." (For what it's worth, our Deep South town of Cleveland lies 33.75° north, 90.72° west.) The playwright calls for very little scenery in the play, and the action relies heavily on miming the interaction with the everyday objects of early 20th century American life. The plot centers on the courtship marriage of Emily Webb and George Gibbs, two high school sweethearts who've grown up beside one another.

The play's final act, Act III, takes place in the cemetery "on a hilltop—a windy hilltop—lots of sky, lots of clouds—often lots of sun and moon and stars." The sky, clouds, moon, stars, and wind must be familiar to the residents of Cleveland's largest cemetery, which lies on the northern outskirts of town, even if hilltops aren't. The audience soon learns that Emily, now Emily Gibbs and wife and mother, has died while giving birth to her second child

Part of the enduring power of the third act lies in the play's tone, which encourages the audience to embrace the illusion that the passage of time will not auger in painful change. It's an illusion dispelled by the presence of the Stage Manager, who is both witness, prophet, and voice of a kind of folksy inevitability, but one most other characters in the play share. The graveyard, into which Emily is brought kicking and screaming to settle into her new life, presents as a dour place, where souls sit stoically in their graves and slowly forget Grover's Corner.

In Act III, Emily Webb decides to go back in time to relive her twelfth birthday against the advice of the older dead of the graveyard. She doesn't make it an hour before she tells the Stage Manager that she can't go on. "It goes so fast. We don't have time to look at one another...I didn't realize. So all that was going on and we never noticed." I know exactly what she means.

Our Emily had just started ninth grade that August, and though, she, like Virginia, presented as older than her fourteen years, she was cast, not as her namesake, but as George Gibbs's bratty sister, Rebecca, whose big scene occurs at the end of Act I. It's night, and George and Rebecca are fighting over who gets to look out at the moon from George's bedroom window. Rebecca tells him of a letter "Jane Crofut got from her minister when she was sick." Playfully, the minister had written on the envelope her address at Crofut Farm to "the universe; the mind of God."

Virginia, who that July had turned eleven, had donated ten inches of the hair that she'd been growing out for two years to Locks of Love, an organization that provides hairpieces to underprivileged children who've suffered hair loss due to disease or medical treatment. Her hair was the shortest it'd been since she was a toddler, and so it was no surprise that she was triple cast as the paperboy brothers, Joe and Si Crowell, and as Emily Webb's little brother, Wally. The development both bemused and amused her, and I joked that if she weren't careful she might get typecast.

"Fine with me," she said defiantly.

Rebecca (Emily) and Wally (Virginia) both end up in the graveyard in the third act, saying little, and looking straight ahead from their chairs, a lot to ask of a talkative sixth grader, who until then had proven constitutionally unable to remain silent for more than five minutes in any setting.

Rehearsing this part of the play proved particularly hard for Virginia, and she surprised and alarmed Emily and the rest of the cast at the first read-through by running off of the stage in tears. When I arrived to pick the girls up that evening, Michael took me aside.

"I don't know what happened. I asked the cast if she said anything, or anyone said anything to her."

Emily was mystified too. Virginia was quiet on the ride home and throughout supper. After she went to her room to finish her homework, I knocked on her door.

"What happened today, baby?" I asked.

She opened her script, which was face down, the front cover holding on for dear life at the edge of the desk. She handed it to me, preserving the open page on which the Stage Manager says: "You know as well as I do that the dead don't stay interested in us living people for very long. Gradually, gradually, they lose hold of the earth...and the ambitions they had...and the pleasures they had...and the things they suffered...and the people they loved."

I understood at once. In the first year after Emily's death, I used to reassure Virginia that, of course, her Mommy was watching her, that we were, in fact, her favorite television show. Her mother switched the channel on the great celestial flat screen over to us whenever she could.

"Can she hear me?" Virginia asked.

"Your mother could do anything," I replied, knowing I was on shaky ground. How do you console a five-year-old without deception? The many books I'd read on the subject hadn't entirely answered the question. Or maybe I just hadn't absorbed the lesson.

"Then why doesn't she talk to me?"

"Maybe she does," I replied, feeling like a cartoon character whose ground has dissolved beneath him. Any second I would plummet to my doom.

"You dream about her, right? Maybe that's her way. She knows how busy you are, so maybe she waits until you're resting."

We talked about it for weeks, at night, as I put her to bed, and in all that time I never told her that Wilder was parroting a prayer I had been saying for years. *Spare Emily the agony of not being here at these moments. Spare my wife the frustration at witnessing my ineptitude at comforting this little girl.* Instead, I turned to the text, defining for Virginia the terms Wilder himself uses when he speaks to the importance of nailing the tone of this final act, especially. "[I]t is important to remove from the picture of the seated dead any suggestion of the morbid or lugubrious. They sit easily.... Emily's revisiting her home and her farewell to the world is under strong emotion, but the emotion is that of wonder rather than sadness." I reminded Virginia of her sister's big scene and told her that her mother's address just had more lines to it now. Her home spiraled out from wherever Virginia and Langston were to Mommy's new home near "the mind of God."

In the six weeks leading up to opening night, Emily and Virginia spent about twenty hours a week in Jobe Hall, the auditorium on campus. Much was down time spent chatting and doing homework, jackets and book bags sprawled over the first rows of seats. Neither had a great number of lines, but both were onstage frequently, in the chorus of the choir and the whole of Act III, so were obliged to be present at rehearsal even when they weren't called upon to say a word.

Our quieter house was strange. Already gone, Katie, our oldest, relished living in her dorm three hours away, and now Emily and Virginia were spending most afternoons and evenings gone. The boys missed their sisters, and our suppers became much more perfunctory. These absences might have proved divisive, further weakening family bonds that had been asserted rather than assumed at the marriage and move three years before, but when I think back on the days of the play, they take on a sort of timelessness, a bubble of family operations in which our relationships seem bound by a stronger force than gravity or inertia.

Thoughts of her mother predominated in Virginia's mind that autumn in the lead up to performance, which was set to coincide almost exactly with the sixth anniversary of Emily's death. Perhaps the dead do slowly forget the worlds they leave behind. Perhaps this is the greatest of nature's mercies. But for those left here, grief works differently. The great sadnesses of our lives stay attached to us. Like a comet, grief returns to us at predictable times—anniversaries, holidays, seasons—but it also catches us up unaware, years after mourning. Something as ephemeral as a scent or a single spoken word, a certain overly familiar atmosphere will bring grief back into our ken, turn us primitive, and invite us to lie down in darkness and hop a ride on its back.

That fall was filled with such moments. Even the mania of the afternoons when I, along with Jennifer, spent so much time getting everyone where they needed to go resonated with that earlier fall of pathological accomplishment when there were no distances I wouldn't travel to obtain or provide for Emily the medicine she needed. I believe that because of the play, the season was more suffused with grief for Virginia than any of the previous falls had been.

The intensity of her grief persisted after the play ended. We spent Thanksgiving at my parents' house in North Carolina and even being in her old room and seeing my parents' cat, Little Bear, couldn't lift her spirits. On the drive home the following Sunday, I decided to try something new. The next day I picked my daughter up from school and, instead of returning home, drove to her favorite restaurant, Guadalajara.

"What's happening?" Virginia asked, cautiously, and I realized that she'd gotten used to hearing bad news when I took her off somewhere by herself.

"Well, you know what day it is, right?" It was December first, the sixth anniversary of Emily's death.

"Yeah," she said, slowly.

"Well, what would they do at Hogwarts on this day?" Virginia had been a Harry Potter fan since second grade and kept her mother's hardbacks of the series on her special shelf. As she'd grown older, her enthusiasm had flamed rather than cooled, and, summers, she spent entire days in the world of wizards and half giants.

I didn't wait for her to answer. I'd made a ritual of marking Emily's birthday every year by giving the children a pin or bracelet or another small trinket from her jewelry box. Emily was fond of animals, so most of the pieces sported bees or bears or otters, making them a hit with even Langston. Now, Virginia and I would celebrate her "Death Day."

"Like Nearly Headless Nick," Virginia said.

"Let's get fried ice cream," I replied, as we pulled into the lot.

Working through grief is lonely work, even if your closest are grieving also. I don't think the fried ice cream helped, but eventually, Virginia became again her usual indomitable self. I knew that wouldn't remain a permanent state, that she'd stumble again under the weight of her loss, but I welcomed her return, and saw it was getting easier for her, for us, even if perspective swung, pendulum-like, in and out of focus.

CLAIMING SPACE

IT'S THE FIRST OF JUNE and I am, as usual, restless. I'm nearing the end of what I call my golden month, the four weeks every year between the semester's end at Delta State University and the last day for the public schools. My wife Jennifer is ready to say goodbye to the fourth grade class she's taught this school year, and our kids are itching to greet their summer. The year is 2014, which means I'm enjoying my fourth such month and regretting, again, that I haven't found a way to make the most of my time. In only three days, school will be out, the kids will not sleep in as long as I hope, and my mornings will no longer be my own. Every year, I'm torn by whether I should embrace this development or not.

Late spring in the Mississippi Delta is an easy time. The wet heat hasn't really seeped in yet, and from the vantage point of my living room windows, every green thing seems to be blooming and every member of the animal kingdom busy with its own becoming. After Jennifer and the kids leave for school, I turn the lights off and delight in the early sun that streams between the slats of the open blinds. I feel like I'm sitting in the shade of an enormous tree. Outside, the business of life, both human and non-human, conducts itself with a persistent and leisurely lack of decorum. Cars amble by, and a loose mongrel lopes along the gutters, exciting the squirrels and nesting birds.

Begun before WWII, my neighborhood has evolved from a straight-line grid of sparsely populated streets to one of a range of house styles and leafy trees. The roads are wide and attract late middle-aged couples who walk their planned patterns in strides that suggest endless time. Sometimes, standing on my front stoop, the breeze is steady in a way that, if I close my eyes, I see the North Carolina beaches of my childhood.

Claiming ownership of the spaces in which she lived was important to my first wife Emily in a way that I never quite acknowledged in our ten years of marriage. We'd moved around so much as adults, living in four states and the District of Columbia, that I'd grown used to thinking of every house or apartment as temporary. But for Emily, the question of whether home was permanent or temporary was irrelevant. Home was always present, always in the present, not an ideal perpetually out of reach or some distorted memory. She gave the impression that she was always where she wanted to be.

My father still laughs about the time we went shopping for a rug to fit our large hallway in our South Carolina bungalow. We'd gone to an outlet about twenty minutes away on I-85. My parents happened to be visiting that weekend, and as we deliberated for hours over hundreds of rugs, they both showed great equanimity—especially my father who spent the time amusing a one year-old Virginia by taking her up and down the escalators of the enormous warehouse. In this respect, my daughter certainly favors me. Even when I know I should sit still and work, I spend my time roaming.

Our home in Mississippi has an odd layout, but I've grown fond of its idiosyncrasies. The simple ranch house was built in 1944, though subsequent owners since expanded the floor plan. Originally, the brick kitchen floor supported a screened porch, and it's said that the inordinately large master suite at the back of the house was a previous resident's clumsy, last-ditch attempt to save his marriage. Looking at it from the top of one of our many pecan trees, the house is shaped like an inverted T, with the arm parallel to the street and the stem dividing the backyard in two. In our single day of house hunting four summers ago it was the only listing in our price range that seemed large enough to accommodate all seven of us. The address is a mile from my office, and I begin each fall term walking to and from work, despite the August heat. By the time October cools things off, the piano and ballet lessons, and soccer and basketball seasons have ended my walks. Every fall I find myself looking forward to the day we will have more eligible drivers in the family, though I know this will mean the house is emptier, too.

Luxuriating in my golden month, I sometimes make a tour of the house, a way of putting off the work I should be doing. I tell myself, as I enter each room, that I'm checking on the cats and the dog, but truthfully, the act is more private ritual than compulsion. Tracking these rooms where so many of the objects are resonant, I feel close to my wife Emily, and to my time with her. Walking toward the front of the house, say, to refill my coffee cup, will lead me to my stepdaughter Emily's room, which had belonged to Katie, our oldest, until last fall, when she left for the Mississippi School for Math and Science. My old bedroom furniture is here, a wedding gift my first wife and I received from her maternal grandmother—and those three pieces may still be the priciest furniture in the house. The deep reddish-brown color of the cherry wood is a little out of place alongside the chronicles of contemporary adolescence that adorn the walls. My stepdaughter Emily celebrates starkness and at the age of fourteen, owns a defensible aesthetic. The scattering of black and white posters and postcards against the white walls are testaments to her love of clean lines and crisp shadows.

The only color besides the furniture is provided by the dozens of family photos arranged chronologically in three separate installments around the room. Images from birthday parties, holiday celebrations, sleepovers, and field trips candidly reveal her toddlerhood, childhood, and early adolescence. The most recent photos are pinned to the bulletin board nearest the bed. Included among them is a series that marks her four month stay at St. Jude, the waves in her long hair grown thin as treatment progressed. In what must be one of the last snapshots from this time, the bright blue wig and straw hat she almost always wore that late spring and summer fails to distract the viewer's gaze from the genuineness of her smile. That Easter, Emily was in the middle of a chemo cycle and though the chemo tired her, she could see the end finally in sight, and the doggedness with which she participated in all the games of the season was inspiring.

The room that Langston and William share is next on my stop, a disorienting transition from Emily's room, given the toys that litter the floor and crowd the shelves and desktops. Langston's glow-in-the-dark mobile of the solar system, a Christmas gift from his godparents, hangs above his bed. He likes to point out that, despite being disqualified as a planet, Pluto is still included, looming large above his pillow as it glows from its spot furthest from the sun.

Stuffed animals and bugs fill his side of the room, which would, I think, please his mother, who was liable to pick up a spider or a mouse with her bare hands as quickly as she might a kitten. The print of the cover of *Goodnight Moon* that she and I had framed for Virginia hangs above his bookshelf, stuffed with all the books we received at Virginia's baby shower. We'd asked for books only and received dozens, including *Emily the Strange*, chosen by a friend from graduate school for mother Emily, not baby Virginia. With its intimations of violence, vaguely vampire-like drawings, and celebration of odd and strong behavior, I try not to worry too much that the book is one of Langston's favorites.

William is eleven, five years older than Langston, and his side of the room is dominated by Lego sets in various states of construction. Once, in an essay on collecting, I wrote that you'll find him most Saturday mornings surrounded by the flat, clear containers that hold the loose pieces he keeps sorted by color and size. He and Langston can spend hours working side by side with the blocks without complaint.

I invariably end up in Virginia's room. Set off from the other bedrooms, it lies beyond the living room. On sunny days, her window and separate backdoor reveal the magnolia tulip, which blooms before spring officially begins. The room is a small space, so small that, when we ordered a loft bed to provide additional floor space, I had to assemble the bed inside the room.

We replaced the large desk built into the other sidewall with a smaller child's desk, but left the built-in bookshelves that go all the way to the ceiling. The shelves are crammed with memorabilia: pictures, small pieces of pottery, a plaster cast of a dog's paw print, and a porcelain statue of a mother and infant that Virginia was given by her mother when she was three, and promptly shattered. The night it fell to a thousand shards Emily and I spent hours with our heads bent over our dining room table, supergluing the statute whole again.

On the top shelf, safely out of reach of her little brother's hands, sit photographs of her mom, and along with two of our old dog, Jane, pictures of Emily when she was young—before Virginia knew her. Centered on the second shelf is the collection of thirty or so shot glasses Emily began bringing home to Virginia when she was called out of town for conferences and interviews. They made perfect fairy glasses and we used to giggle mischievously to each other when Virginia brought them out on play dates. In one corner rests a wooden clock the two of them spent a Saturday constructing from a kit.

Nearby on the wall hangs a photograph of Emily from our wedding. She looks out from that picture at a poster of Harry Potter and a map of the world. Suspended from the top windowsill is the sun piñata from Virginia's fourth birthday—intact because she couldn't stand the thought of someone swinging a stick at it.

A small writing desk sits under the loft bed and beside it a slim bookcase that Emily kept within an arm's reach of our bed, on which she stored all the beloved books of her childhood. Virginia has added a few books to that collection, including a copy of her mother's book and a couple of my poetry collections. The bookcase also holds multiple hand-sewn editions of the series of bear poems I began making when Virginia was three. *The Book of Bear* has now expanded to become *The Book of Bear, Otter, and Armadillo*. Every couple of years we'll give the latest edition to the teachers of our three youngest. Most of the books, though, date from her mother's childhood: the set of C.S. Lewis's *Chronicles of Narnia*, yellowing in its yellow gift box, the cloth hardbacks of the Laura Ingalls Wilder books whose spines had ruptured and whose covers have shredded from years and use.

My daughter still sleeps on Ump, the giant frog she received from Santa when she was two. Ump sits level with my eye on top of the loft bed, and I always catch his wide smile when I turn to leave. On her new desk, Virginia has placed the headshot the Georgetown Theology Department took of Emily for their website and brochure.

Emily, with her genuine smile, is radiant before the sterile, gray-blue background. Beside the photograph, Virginia keeps a small clay Madonna and child from Peru that Emily always liked. This Mary works in the fields and carries her baby on her back. Both mother and child have turned their heads to one side, as if caught mid-stride, never seeming to meet my gaze, always looking down and away.

Eleven-year-old Virginia has matured quickly and can now wear some of her mother's clothes, so even a glance at her closet thrusts me back through time. The bed sheets are covered with the quilt that a kind neighbor in D.C. made from Emily's favorite outfits, patchwork glimpses of favorite sweaters and pants that remain on the bed no matter how mercilessly the Mississippi sun beats down upon us.

Like most girls her age Virginia can feel aggrieved by her parents or siblings, and at those times, retreats to this room and slams her door. Sometimes, between sobs, I hear her appeal loudly to her mother, and it's taken me years to learn to resist the urge to rush in and comfort her, partly because I too, on occasion, have prayed aloud to Emily in this room. In the rawness of that first year after Emily's death, it was comforting to be surrounded by her things, then, as now, most heavily concentrated wherever Virginia rests her head. Only last year, I fell asleep on the floor one afternoon, Virginia's photo album spread over my chest, only to start awake when I heard the long screech of the school bus's brakes.

Too often I respond to Virginia's displays of periodic grief by bestowing on her some new relic of her mother in a quick, clumsy attempt to soothe her. Of course, I'm really merely buying time, forestalling the cycle of pain she'll face her entire life. Eventually, there won't be anything left for me to give as shore against her grief.

When our oldest daughter, Katie, began the program at the Mississippi School for Math and Science, housed at the University for Women three hours away, we offered her room to Virginia, but she refused to leave her tree, her shelves. She felt even the walls of her room would miss her. I understood. The sensation I feel when I move to the center of her little space is agreeably unsettling. At the periphery I pick up fragments of the images and tokens of her mother.

As I move, they seem to connect to me. If I dreamed this, I might see strands of different colored light, a kaleidoscopic web of juxtaposition and configuration reaching me from all directions.

Visiting this room is yet another way I've found to bend time. I'll catch sight of the framed photograph of Emily Dickinson's grave on Virginia's top shelf and snap back to our two-room apartment on Cedar Street in Greensboro, where we'd hastily relocated in our first year of marriage so that Emily could focus on applying to PhD programs. The photograph stood on our shared desk in the front room, where, in those days, we took turns working on our own projects between shifts at the bookstore and restaurant.

Inside the frame with the photograph is a pressed buttercup Emily's family surreptitiously picked from Dickinson's gravesite. Her parents had taken Emily on a tour of New England the summer before she started high school and gave her the photo the following Christmas. Above the photograph, her father typed the following caption: In early June, 1884, Emily Dickinson wrote, "*When it shall come my turn, I want a buttercup—Doubtless the Grass will give me one, for does she not revere the whims of her flitting children.*" One hundred and one years and one month later, he noted that a buttercup *was picked for her namesake, Emily Arndt, on 20 July, 1985.*

In that first year of our marriage, Emily filled the two rooms of the apartment on Cedar Street with hanging vines and broad-leafed potted plants and trees, and, sometimes, looking at the photograph and pressed buttercup on Virginia's shelf, I don't have to close my eyes to see those greens and to breathe the oxygen-enriched air.

Hallowed ground. Will I find it in the actual places of Emily's past or the things that survive to give these new spaces contour and color? I think of those geographies that she so effortlessly held dear: the stream by the park near her childhood home where she caught crayfish with her childhood friend, Kelly; the pure beaches and animal trails of Bald Head Island when there were only a dozen houses from one end of the island to the other; the creek-filled mountain forests around Asheville, her college home; the James River outside Roanoke, where I baptized our dog, Jane, in the lazy current soon after our marriage began; the labyrinth beside the Episcopal church in Wilkesboro, where we buried our child that could not be before Langston was born. I like to think these are the places she went in the silences of our last fall together. I like to think she is there now.

To Wait with the Pigeons to Wake

Such stuff as dreams are made on

—Prospero, *The Tempest*

It took six and a half years for my mind to leave Georgetown Hospital, six and a half years for certain memories of those eighteen months in D.C. to find their way back to the surface of my dreams. I know these memories have suffered a bit, as I have suffered. I've undergone a sea change—it's a pearl now that was once my mind's blinking eye.

Our apartment on 39th Street was on the second of a three-story "garden style" building. I have an image in my head from our first year there, of Emily sitting at the end of the dining room table that was too long for our four-room apartment. It must have been a Sunday. She was drinking coffee and eating a chocolate croissant from Whole Foods. Her laptop, on the hard drive of which her not-quite-finished book was saved, was open. Books and papers lay scattered around her. Virginia sat on the floor by the coffee table, playing with Star Wars figures. I know Emily's croissant was chocolate because I was as obsessive about new foods as Virginia was about new toys. I'd discovered the croissants our first week in D.C. and brought them back that morning after taking the dog for her morning walk.

The table spanned the double window along the outside wall of our central room. It just fit, but there was only enough space to sit at the kitchen end, the end that later served us so well the following year when, in the last two months of Emily's life, I had to administer the heavy antibiotics through her I.V. I needed the large area on which to place the sterilizing supplies and medicine, and Emily needed the hard back of the dining room chair to hold her upright for the procedure. Luckily, those memories don't obliterate the image of that weekend morning.

The table was an imprudent purchase our first semester of graduate school, when we were flush with our first stipend checks and wanted to at last feel like adults in our own home. We went to Pier One and bought it on the spot, a mission-style of dark grain, almost black, a display model with four chairs and a bench. The purchase still makes me proud, though, it wasn't until years later, when Emily accepted her first teaching job at Converse College in Spartanburg, South Carolina, that we lived in a house large enough to accommodate our dining room set. The restored Arts and Crafts bungalow, with its five fireplaces, twelve foot ceilings and great hall, welcomed our long table. Before that, we'd eaten most of our meals on the couch before a small aluminum outdoor table, a remainder from one of Emily's exes that today holds our eleven-year-old daughter's books of mythology and spell in her bedroom. The big table, scarred from the claws of our dog, Jane, remains with me, too, and finally serves a family large enough to fit all seven of its seats.

In that memory of that Sunday morning, it must have been mid-morning, early in the 2006 fall semester, because Emily wasn't mulling over her classes but was thinking about the dissertation she planned to turn into her ticket to tenure. She wasn't yet pregnant with Langston, though we'd been thinking about him, about who he might be and how complete he would make us feel. Now that Emily had completed her PhD and landed a job that might sustain her for her career, she again thought about giving Virginia a sibling. Emily had been an only child and wanted to spare her daughter the loneliness of being the only source of parental aspiration and disappointment.

I'd secretly, passively, resisted having another child, perfectly and joyfully overwhelmed by four-year-old Virginia, who, almost since birth, seemed a force of nature and was the only person able to bring me out of myself no matter my mood. Because our apartment was half the size of our South Carolina bungalow, Virginia and I had begun taking weekend excursions. Perhaps that morning Virginia, Jane, and I were hoping for a walk on the trails of the National Forest that covered our neighborhood. We played Hobbits, roaming the woods as Bilbo and Bilbino—my made-up name for Virginia—splashing in the creek and climbing on the ship's-rope vines that dangled over the trails, oblivious to the activity and excitement of a major city three blocks away.

At the time everything new seemed an independent miracle: my eleventh-hour job, the spot for Virginia that opened up one week before school started in the second Pre-K classroom at Stoddert Elementary, an old-fashioned, red-brick schoolhouse that had drawn our attention immediately when we were looking for apartments: the prospect of a school so close to home had made our choice of home an easy one. Effortlessly, everything had fallen into place and I began to wake each morning expecting to be delighted by a new discovery. On Saturdays that September, Emily and Virginia headed downtown to the National Museum for free art lessons and scavenger hunts while I spent the morning writing—first with coffee in bed, then at one of the picnic tables near Stoddert within view of the D2 bus from Dupont Circle, which Virginia and I called the R2D2. I loved watching my wife and daughter walk across that field to meet me after their adventures, as they called their activities.

It's remarkable how successfully even the conscious mind bends time. Sometimes, hearing my wife's lovely voice in a different part of the house, I still have to remind myself that the voice is that of my second wife Jennifer, not Emily. Jennifer views parenthood the way Emily did, and Emily, also, possessed Jennifer's way of instinctively negotiating the everyday. Both had the ability be at home anywhere, which helps me believe that they might have been friends, my very own Hermia and Helena. Lucky dreaming me.

After Emily's death, I hadn't been able to claim my dreams as my own. When I dreamed of childhood, I dreamed of Virginia's childhood before her mother's death. Or I dreamed of Langston's childhood in a world that should have been. A couple years ago, as I was preparing for my two-year tenure review, I dreamed that Emily had been denied tenure. The dream woke me, but then I fell asleep again and dreamed that she was the department chair to whom I was making my i-dotted, t-crossed case. I woke fully, and promptly decided to invest in a binder for my portfolio, anticipating how exhaustive my plea would have to be.

The tenure dream had been only the third dream I'd had of Emily in the four years following her death. Virginia has been graced with visits from her mother much more often, a phenomenon for which I'm happy, mostly. The mother of Langston's godmother, a practicing Buddhist, once told me that people who suffer early deaths ascend higher on the ladder toward enlightenment, and I sometimes fear that Emily visits me so infrequently because I feel so far from any sense of enlightenment.

Emily was so generous with her students, so careful and so gifted a teacher, yet I can easily see her having done something else with her life. Once, after waking in the hospital, she turned to me and said she thought she'd like to go to the Appalachian mountains and work with her hands, become a potter in Asheville, where she'd gone to college and first fallen in love with her life. I assumed she'd been dreaming of a place as far away from that hospital room as she could imagine, but last summer, while visiting her parents, I found a photo of her in our high school yearbook. She's sculpting a figure in clay, and though she was often self-conscious about having her picture taken, the camera caught her wholly absorbed in her work. If teaching hadn't worked out for her somehow, becoming a potter might have made for a satisfactory back-up plan.

In the first dream I'd had of Emily after her death, we were strangers to each other. She was younger than I'd known her, as young as in the yearbook picture, and we were in what felt like New York City. She wore a green pea coat with the collar turned up against the winter wind, and I couldn't quite make out her face. I had to meet her so I chased after her on the street. The world was all cement and abstract silver faces and I couldn't get close enough to capture her attention. I fell down a pothole and woke enough to dream a ladder at the end of the tunnel, rising to the street and found I'd gained ground. But I never caught her. She disappeared over the broad steps of an institutional building, which might have been the public library, the famous one with the lions. In the dream I was unable to climb the steps. I could only sit on a bench across the street and wait with the pigeons to wake up.

Both the winters in New York and the pea coat were part of our actual history together. Six months after Emily and I met as coworkers at the independent bookstore in our hometown, Emily began her graduate work at Fordham University in the heart of the Bronx while I finished up my final year at the University of North Carolina at Greensboro, still unsure about almost everything in my life. Unsure about everything but Emily. After I'd proposed on her visit back home for Thanksgiving, I'd gone up to New York to see her, skipping the last of my classes that semester and mailing in my few final papers. We spent most of the winter break in her apartment on 187th Street, eating pizza, watching bad television with her roommate, and sleeping late. Occasionally, we emerged from our nest to recognize that we were in a rather large city filled with people, and to buy Christmas presents in Greenwich Village.

My second dream was the most painful. I'd been remarried almost a year, a difficult year during which my stepdaughter had been diagnosed and treated for a germ cell tumor, and I'd just finished up my first year of teaching in a new state. Like the rest of my new blended family of seven, I was learning how to negotiate our new terrain. Though we'd lived in Mississippi for eleven months, I wondered if any of us would learn to speak the language of the place.

My Emily chose to visit me a hot July night just as the summer school term was beginning. She tucked me into bed, as if I were sick, then moved to the door, turned, and snapped her fingers playfully when I asked her, angrily, to stay.

"So we're doing this now?" she asked with one of her knowing smiles.

"No. That's her," I said, jabbing my thumb toward the blanketed form beside me that I took to be Jennifer sleeping on her side of the bed. Even my dream self knew I was being petulant, a child.

"I like it. Do you remember how I used to..." she began, shaking her finger in mock anger.

"Yes. Insazy." *Insazy* had been part of our marital lexicon, an endearing example of Emily's habit, usually in moments of great feeling, of unconsciously creating portmanteaus. "Crazy" and "insane." Nothing could dispel an argument between us faster than *insazy*.

"How can you stay?" I asked her.

When I asked again, she vanished, and I was outside myself, looking down, as if the face beneath me were my reflection, but the eyes of my mirror self were closed. My lips pursed, as if waiting to be kissed.

Mystery. It's our magical ignorance of our own brains that makes the images they create resonate through our lives and makes our dreams a subject of fascination and study. Most assume our dreams, even the bad ones, are trying to do us good: dreams occur to solve the problems that vex our waking lives or to clean out the stuff of the past so that we can solve our problems in the clear light of tomorrow. But I prefer ideas that avoid mere reason. Dreams as visitations. Dreams as wishes, desires that lie deeply enough that they're beyond our control. Can you choose with whom you fall in love? Would you want to? Jung called them big, the big dreams, the ones in which your apprehension seems quickened, more alive, as if your mind's eye comprehended more than the usual spectrum of life, as if you'd been loaned crow's eyes, wolf's snout, hare's ears.

One morning this past fall, I woke thinking of that fall in D.C. ten years ago, the fall before it all fell so terribly, a time when the idea of having another child was still a private one, one that Emily and I discussed late at night so that Virginia, a notoriously difficult sleeper, couldn't hear. I remembered Halloween. Our neighborhood Glover Park, with an odd mixture of small and large families, students, teachers, and young professionals, embraced Halloween like no other we'd known.

As the day darkened, we stepped to the corner and were swept away by a rush of costume and merriment. Neighbors kept beer coolers on their porches, so the parents went trick-or-treating, too. It took us three blocks to find our feet and plan our route around the neighborhood, and, an hour later, we'd all three had enough. I recall thinking, as I lay in bed and tried to prolong the reverie, of how warm and glowing our central room had seemed as Emily, Virginia, and I sat cross-legged on the floor with Virginia's Halloween loot piled in the center.

Luxuriating in the memory, I found that, for once, I wasn't trying to fix things. I could think of that time without trying to construct a way out, to look for something I'd missed the first time, or uncover some clue to Emily's health that might have changed things for her, for all of us. I knew that as soon as Christmas, our story would begin to spiral downward. Each time that I'd begin to remember the merest detail of those eighteen months in D.C., I'd had to close my eyes to that past life. Not so this morning. Time brought me back to the present, warm in my bed in Mississippi, with my love Jennifer still sleeping beside me, my eyes wide open.

NOTES

Arndt, Emily. *Demanding Our Attention.* Eerdmanns: Grand Rapids, MI, 2011.

Auden, W.H. *Collected Poems.* New York: Vintage International, 1991.

Didion Joan. *The Year of Magical Thinking.* Vintage, 2007.

Garland, Robert. *The Greek Way of Death.* Cornell University Press, 2001.

Hoffman, Yoel, ed. *Japanese Death Poems: Written by Zen Monks and Haiku Poets on the Verge of Death.* Tuttle Publishing, 1998.

Hollander, John. *Selected Poetry.* New York: Alfred A Knopf, 1997.

Hughes, Langston. *The Collected Poems of Langston Hughes.* New York: Vintage Classics, 1994.

Lindsay, Vachel. *General William Booth Enters Into Heaven, and Other Poems.* The Macmillan Company, 1913.

Wilder, Thornton. *Our Town.* Samuel French, Inc. New York, 2013.

ACKNOWLEDGMENTS

No amount of gratitude can properly account for the generosity and kindness of the people who surrounded us that summer and fall in Washington, D.C.

I want to thank the people that make up Georgetown University, the students that volunteered their time to hang out with Virginia and Langston, Emily's colleagues in the Theology Department, among them, Jonathan Ray, Terrence Reynolds, Julia Lamm, and Theresa Sanders, university administrators who went beyond even reasonable expectations of stewardship both before and after Emily's death.

Our neighbors in Glover Park: Julie and Rick Schneider, Marta Beresin and Bill Scher, Alec and Lely McKay, and Ali Nabavi were indispensable, as were Virginia's godparents Brandon Nelson and Marsaura Shukla, and Langston's godparents, Lahra Smith and Dawit Zegeye. Emily's friends from grad school who came to stay and look after us all kept me sane in crucial moments and the children clothed, fed, and entertained, among them Michelle Rubio, Carla Ingrando, and Nancy Johnson.

I am grateful to Emily's mentor Jean Porter and our friends from Notre Dame who were so helpful and sustaining to me then, and again when I began this project: Valerie Sayers and Chris Jara, John and Diana Matthias, William O'Rourke and Steve and Maria Tomasula, Tony D'Souza, and Jenny Boully. I also want to thank our friends and colleagues from graduate school, college, and high school, and our friends and neighbors in Spartanburg and Greensboro, who let us know that although we had moved away, we stayed close in their good thoughts.

Most of all, I want to thank my parents, grandparents, brothers, and sister-in-law, without whom I would still be lost.

Three years later, I was again shown the importance of community and friendship while my stepdaughter underwent treatment. Friends such as Laura Joost, Bill and Jeanne Hays, were a great help to us that spring, as were the members of St. Paul's Episcopal Church in Cary, North Carolina, the Margaret Green Junior High School student council, and the members of Calvary Episcopal Church in Cleveland. I want also to thank Mike Paup, Julie Fowler, and Anne Barnhill, who came to stay and help at crucial times.

Finally, I am very grateful to the editors who encouraged me in writing the essays of this book and first published some of them, often in different versions. *Notre Dame Magazine* first published "My Emilys" as "My Two Emilys"; *Chattahoochee Review* published "Gifts She Named Mine" as "Langston"; *Image* published "Pigeons and Turtledoves"; *storySouth* published "To Wait with the Pigeons and Wake" as "Such Stuff"; and "Shadow Texts" first appeared in *Witness* and was republished in the anthology *Done Darkness: An Anthology about Life Beyond Sadness*. I also want to thank the Mississippi Arts Commission for awarding me a literature fellowship that allowed me to embark on this project.

Early readers of these essays helped me organize my scattered thoughts, and I want to thank Anne Clinard Barnhill, Michael Ewing, Stacy Cartledge, Edward Plough, Jason Smith, and Brandon Nelson for their advice and encouragement. Most of all, I want thank WTAW Press and its founder Peg Alford Pursell, who took a chance on this manuscript and worked tirelessly to give it its final shape. I remain grateful for her advocacy.

ABOUT THE AUTHOR

A native of Philippi, West Virginia, Mike Smith is a graduate of UNC-G, Hollins College, and the University of Notre Dame. He has

published three collections of poetry, including *Multiverse*, a collection of two anagrammatic cycles. His translation of the first part of Goethe's *Faust* was published by Shearsman Books in 2012, and he is co-editor of the anthology, *The Mint's Invitation: Contemporary Chinese Short-Shorts in Translation*, forthcoming from Columbia University Press in the fall of 2017. Together with software engineer Brandon Nelson, Smith created and curates *The Zombie Poetry Project* at www.zombiepoetryproject.com.

WTAW Press is a 501 (c) 3 nonprofit press and thanks the following supporters for their assistance.

Anonymous	Molly Giles	Cheryl Morris
Maria Benet	Mark Goldrosen	Ginger Murchison
Rosaleen Bertolino	Gary Hawkins	John Phillip
Amanda Conran	Patrick Hayes	Anne Raeff
Walter B. Doll	Dorothy Hearst	Marleen Roggow
Audrey Ferber	Mary Herr	Aran Ramsey Tate
Charlene Finn	Leslie Ingham	Anne Taylor
DB Finnegan	Susan Ito	Elizabeth Terzakis
Gerald Fleming	Scott Landers	Janet Thornburg
Rebecca Foust	Richard May	Debra Turner
Joan Frank	Denise Miller	Townsend Walker
Stephanie Fuelling	Alison Moore	Olga Zilberbourg